"Anyone lucky enough to have worked with L   what an engaging, clever leader he is. His new book *Exponential Leadership* reflects these core strengths by delivering deep insight through compelling storytelling. All business leaders can benefit by reading along with the narrator's journey and by applying Doug's simple but effective leadership formula. Both teams and organizations will benefit greatly!"
— Amy Collins, Vice President, Team Experience, Payoff

"A refreshing read that, unlike so many other leadership books, does not lecture its readers how to be an impactful leader but instead really gets them thinking about the interworking dynamics of all the elements that go into effective and impactful leadership. A wonderful and easy read that manages to keep you on the edge of your seat – you'll want to know what the final 'Leadership Equation' looks like! -- *Exponential Leadership* helps you explore your own leadership philosophy and open your mind to new possibilities."
— Mike O'Brien, SVP, Regional Director (Americas), Euler Hermes

"*Exponential Leadership* is filled with real examples of business challenges that resonate with practical advice that all leaders can employ in both their personal and professional lives. After reading this book, new and experienced leaders alike will make more and better decisions that translate into impactful results."
— Marc Farrugia, Vice President, Human Resources, Sun Communities & Sun RV Resorts

"Exponential Leadership by Doug Johnston is so cleverly written that I found myself in a virtual reality mode being a part of the story. The characters come to life and the message is crystal clear. Whether novice or seasoned leader, Doug reminds us that lifelong learning is THE mindset to adopt in order to have a lasting impact."
— Joey Persico, Senior Director for Human Resources and USCG Veteran

"Doug Johnston's book is a great and thought-provoking read. It came my way in a very timely manner as I endeavor to lead a large CPA firm. Accurately reflecting the experiences of any leader, it is truly eye-opening with regard to what each of us can do to produce truly impactful results. I plan to read this book again and again!"
— Kevin C. Hill, CPA, Chief Executive Officer, EFPR Group, LLP

"Exponential Leadership epitomizes author Doug Johnston's approach to leadership development, blending strategy, practicality, and learning moments in a manner that all leaders can relate to. It's a book that challenges its readers to be more naturally curious and to consider what a lasting impact really looks like."
— Craig Klebe, Director, Business Transformation

e^{x}ponential LEADERSHIP

Formulating YOUR Impact

DOUG JOHNSTON

Published by Impact4Results Books
Doug Johnston, President
dougj@impact4results.com
impact4results.com

Design and Graphics by
Cindy Murphy, Bluemoon Graphics

Ordering Information:
Special discounts are available on quantity purchases by corporations, associations, and others. For details, contact the publisher at the address above.

ISBN-13: 978-1975956721
ISBN-10: 1975956729

Library of Congress Control Number: PENDING
CreateSpace Independent Publishing Platform, North Charleston, SC

LCCN Imprint Name: Impact4Results Books, Victor, New York

Contents

*e*^{x}ponential LEADERSHIP

Dedication

To Francine, the love of my life and unwavering supporter. I couldn't have done this without your unconditional and enthusiastic support.

To my children Emily and David, my inspiration. I said from the start that if I write this book and you are the only ones who read it, I will have accomplished my goal. I share with you something deeply personal and important to me, and here I pass it on to you.

Acknowledgements

How do you acknowledge all the people who get you to where you are going? There are so many that have influenced me in finishing this project. So please forgive me if I leave someone off this list.

First to my wife Francine who has listened to me talk about doing this for so long. "Hey Honey, I am done!" Your belief in me, your encouragement, and your support are far more than anyone can ask for. You read, you listened, you shared ideas, you edited and most importantly encouraged. You are my true partner in this.

To my friend Joey, you took an interest in this from the start and asked me to continue to send sections as I finished them. Outside of my immediate team, you saw this long before anyone else. Your interest and encouragement were rocket fuel to me.

To my publishing team, Ken, Elena and Cindy. I can't tell you how much you have shaped this book and how you have shaped me. First the encouragement propelled me through the process. Your feedback always helpful. You guided me from draft to final product, resulting in a book that I am truly proud of and that I hope you are equally proud of.

To John M. for believing in this enough to put your handprint on this book and sharing your thoughts and insights with these readers.

To all of those who took the time to read the rough manuscript and provided testimonials: Amy C., Craig K., Dan H., Gary D., Joey P., Kevin H., Marc F., and Mike O.

There are so many friends who encouraged me and listened to me talk about this (maybe ad nauseum). You offered support, encouragement and confidence. So many of you believed in me when I didn't. Those gestures, no matter how small, helped me more than you will know. I can't name everyone, and there were many, but here are a few: Rob C., Tom M., Hannah M., Dan H., Kevin H., Gary D., Craig K., Lisa C., Mark S, LJ R, and Scott M.

To my sister Betty Sue who got me interested in serious reading, giving me great authors and interesting stories to read. Consuming those titles over the years ultimately inspired me in this endeavor. Without those as fodder I would have probably had to write this book in crayon and it would have much, much shorter.

There are so many relationships since I started my advisory firm in 2002 who inspired the ideas and stories in this book, whether one of my valued clients, workshop participants, people I have worked with on strategic planning or special projects, people that have approached me after a keynote and of course my former Vistage colleagues (think tank group members, fellow chairpersons and speakers). Each helped shape my thinking, and what I learned helped form some of the foundations for the stories in this book. A special shout

out to my friend Brian F. who I hope sees this from above and knows how he has been with me throughout this and will always be with me. I wish I could enjoy one more of our marathon lunches or dinners so I could celebrate this with you.

There are so many people that have crossed my path professionally that I now consider to be friends. The list is long. The generosity of sharing your knowledge, your experience and your support over the years has meant so much.

To those I have worked with, worked for and have worked for me. All of our experiences together shaped me in one way or another. As a result, your handprints are all over this book.

Last, but certainly not least, to God. Although I've struggled with my faith while writing this book, I have no question in my mind that somehow your divine influence and inspiration got me here. There is no other explanation for how this book flowed onto the page with a voice all its own.

Foreword

by John McLaren

I believe that no matter your level of responsibility, your experience as a leader or your knowledge of business, Doug Johnston's *Exponential Leadership* will guide you in making a lasting **impact** by creating **focus**, building **interrelationships** and being deliberate about the beliefs that create a great **culture**. I found so many places where this book reflected my own experiences and the challenges and opportunities that my team faces every day.

Let me share a few reflections of our experiences at Sun Communities and how this book connected for me.

The following statements are central to our culture at Sun Communities:

"We are an inspired, engaged, and collaborative team committed to providing extraordinary service for our residents, guests, and each other."

"Treat others the way you wish to be treated."

These were written by our team, and have been our company's Vision and Service Statements expressing our philosophies since 2009. They continue to be a part of our core foundation, reminding us of whom we strive to be and ultimately supporting all that we do.

Many companies have statements such as these and unfortunately in many cases those statements feel hollow. I would be the first to say that we are not perfect at executing under our own philosophies but that is not the objective. Instead, our objective is to remain on the journey with a cultural feeling and a faith that goes beyond the above statements – a **culture** of continual learning, leading to continual growth one forward step at a time, but with little regard to how big or small the step may be. Just as long as we keep moving forward.

What about results?

I remember one instance when we at Sun Communities were addressing a particularly daunting challenge. It was December 15th, the year was closing, and all the historical data we had in our spreadsheets indicated that we would not achieve one of our most important goals for the year unless we performed like we never had before.

We were in the middle of our two-day quarterly operations team meetings, and on the night between the two days I remember laying wide awake in bed, thinking, "There is not much time. And there simply has to be a way."

Certainly all of us were in sync with the result we wanted, and as a team we knew that we could accomplish great things if we only put our minds to it. But we just didn't quite know how to go about achieving it.

Not really knowing why, I next found myself sitting at the dining room table at 1 AM writing multiple call guides. While doing this, an idea started to formulate.

"Many hands makes for lighter work," I thought to myself, "and we have a whole **culture** that is truly committed to our journey."

The plan was organized and the next morning I presented my idea—not just to the operations team but to the whole company. So we scrapped the original meeting agenda and instead discussed where we stood in relation to our commitment to the **impact** we wanted to have in the remaining days of the year.

I asked for volunteers everywhere in the company to pick up a call guide, and a list of customers, in order to set appointments for our community teams. They would become a direct participant in achieving the result. It was very, very exciting and I was delighted to see that we had many volunteers.

Many of our volunteers came from unexpected areas of the firm such as Accounts Payable, Admin, IT and HR. For many, this was actually the first time they had ever made calls like this, so they were understandably nervous! But as our team volunteers got on the phone with the call guides that day, their nervous jitters quickly melted away, replaced by success.

Even more remarkable was how effectively everyone communicated across the company, inspiring each other and celebrating our results. It ultimately became a movement that couldn't be stopped, during a time of year most believed could only be a slow period for our type of business.

When we closed the year, we hadn't just achieved our objective unsupported by data, but we beat the objective by nearly 10%. More importantly, we had taken a step in shattering the status quo. Now we had a victory to build upon that demonstrated the immeasurable value of our relationships with each other, and a remarkable impact our organizational faith and **beliefs** could have on our final results.

Once again, we are hardly perfect, and we humbly continue taking steps on the path. But because of that challenge years ago, my reading *Exponential Leadership* rang very familiar to me, feeling as though I was sitting in my own office. I am certain this book's main character, Jeff, will be as relatable a figure for many other leaders as he was for me. I have had many of the very same conversations as Jeff, continually searching for an "equation" that embodies who I want to be as a leader, and moreover, what my company culture wants to be.

All too often, people mistake management with leadership, electing command over collaboration. These sorts of mistakes are toxic and can quickly erode the inspiration and creativity needed for cultures to thrive and realize previously unimagined impact and results. In his book, Doug challenges us to ask ourselves tough questions like:

> *What are our Highest Impact Pursuits and what if they were all aligned?*
>
> *What Focused Actions can we take to create Impactful Results?*
>
> *What if we had the courage to build a web and look inward and outward, examining our relationships and key connections with our partners and each other?*

*What if we examined the relationship between Beliefs
and Culture?*

What's more, Doug presents Jeff and the challenges
he faces in an interesting, storytelling way. I have read
many books over the course of my career on the topics
of business and leadership. Many of these reads offer a
more step-by-step in approach, leaving out the human
element of leadership. *Exponential Leadership* is one of
the very few where I could actually feel the concerns,
frustrations, cares, and joys that our leader experienced
all along his journey. It's a book that is well worth your
time. While reading it, you, like I, will feel as though you
are actually there.

Because like me, perhaps you have been! And also like
me, perhaps you will be there again! Most of us who
have a responsibility to lead will be there again and again
but this time, with the help of Doug's book, we will know
how to proceed.

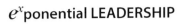

e^xponential LEADERSHIP

Introduction

Every writer will tell you about the challenges of writing a book. In many cases the most significant barrier is self-doubt. I drank from that cup far too often. What I found to be the antidote to self-doubt was purpose. I was able to move past this only by assigning some personal meaning to what I was doing. To that end, I had to answer the question of why I wrote this book and what "impact" I wanted to have.

First, like anyone who writes, I felt I had something to say. Not something definitive or the ultimate answer to the questions of the universe. I thought I had something to say that might shape how we lead.

I have had the privilege of working with and leading others in business before I started my own advisory firm in 2002.

In my advisory practice, one of the common phrases that is unsettling to me is that all of this leadership and communication "stuff" is all soft skills. I hear words like amorphous, touchy feely, immeasurable. Too often attempts to build leadership and communication get quickly shoved aside by the tyranny of operational priorities. Damn the torpedoes, hit the numbers.

If we are honest with ourselves, we will admit that each of us has said and done things we later realized were not the most effective—in fact, they may have even been damaging—course of action in the name of being expeditious. We have also watched others, or enabled others, to wreak havoc because they get things done. It is easy to focus on raw production at the expense of building a sustainable leadership culture throughout the organization.

To a certain degree much of this leadership and communication "stuff" is immeasurable. Of course we have measurements from personality and style assessments, to engagement surveys, and employee surveys. Don't get me wrong; they are important. However, having taken enough graduate-level statistics to be dangerous, we have to admit that we can only explain a fraction of the variability between these measurements and actual business success. That means for all these great measurements, they aren't sufficient to predict what is causing someone to be successful. There is far more to success that is out in the ether.

I've also been unsettled by the number of books by business leaders who claim to have the magic solution—and we believe them. I have read many such books. They are interesting and insightful, but the challenges and solutions they face are usually out of the reaches of what most of us face every day. Chances are I am not going to be piloting a major corporation through the seas of change. So application becomes difficult when I think about their journey versus my own.

There are nearly a quarter of a million books on Amazon related to the topic of leadership alone. Do we really need one more? I came to believe that we do. Not because there are things that haven't been said yet. Google estimates there are 130 million books that have been published. I have to assume that everything that could be said, has been said somewhere.

In this book I draw some correlations between theoretical physics and leadership. A similar search on Amazon shows that there are about as many books on physics as there are on leadership. This means we are continuing to explore on a deep level how our world and the universe works. I think most of us would admit that is a worthy endeavor. Similarly, we should continue to explore leadership and communication and what they mean to us. They say we only understand and can explain about 5% of the universe. I would suggest we only understand a fraction of what leadership and communication really means and how they drive results.

I think each book provides us with an opportunity to explore more deeply those things that are important to us. Sometimes we read something that is written in such a way that it resonates in our hearts and minds. Other times we read something similar to what we have read before, but it is something that is contemporary to the challenges we are facing at that moment, so it is much more applicable for that reason. The key is to read on and see what speaks to you.

It is my hope that this book provides more fodder to anyone that wants to continue to explore. Maybe we should draw from the world of physics and what they call the greats like Albert Einstein, Carl Sagan and yes Sheldon, from *The Big Bang Theory*. They call these great thinkers "theoretical physicists." Maybe we should consider ourselves theoretical leaders. It seems when we don the title of "leader," it implies we have the answer. The reality is we spend our lifetime figuring it out.

That is what leads to the definition of the Leadership Equation discussed in this book. I was thinking about the theory of relativity and how Einstein created a very simple and elegant formula to help scientists unpack the universe. What is underneath $E=MC^2$ is very complex yet he distilled it down into a framework we still use today to understand the relationship between the important elements of our universe.

By way of disclaimer, I have no background in physics and my knowledge ends at drawing the correlation between the theory of relativity and the equation I propose here. I did however read a book called $E=MC^2$: *The Biography Of The World's Most Famous Equation* by David Bodanis. I will humbly admit that it only revealed how much I don't know.

But it also served as a humble reminder about the gaps in my knowledge about leadership. It is my hope that this equation helps me, and you as the reader, to explore leadership, to discover the relationship between what we do and the results we get so that we can have a greater impact on the world around us. By thinking about leadership and communication as an equation it might show us that, although difficult to measure, these topics are not soft skills, immeasurable and amorphous. That if we could wave a magic wand, we could find a way to quantify and measure leadership in a more definitive way.

Until that day comes, I hope that this book provides you with a framework to aid in your exploration.

I chose to write this book as a story because I find any story to be interesting. We are by nature storytellers and we tend to remember the stories that have the lessons embedded in them. I hoped to entertain while trying to provide something that would spark inspiration. I did provide some tools for each part of the equation to start the process of exploration. These, I hope, will serve as a reference as you continue to unpack your own leadership impact.

I invite you to sit back, put your feet up and follow along in the journey of our characters and see where it may lead you. I am honored you would allow this story to come into your life.

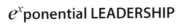

Chapter *1*

What Are We Solving For?

It was another one of those flat forehead nights. Meaning, those nights, after everyone had left for the day, where I would bang my head against the top of my desk until my forehead felt bruised and flattened. There had been too many of these nights. I'm surrounded by dark offices and shadowy hallways. Only a dim desk lamp illuminates my own office. In the still that settles in the twilight, the only sounds are the groaning of the heating or air conditioning and the wobbling warble of wheels of the cleaning service carts as they make their way through the hallways collecting the remnants of another frantic day.

I occupy that hallowed corner office, asked to run this division after a successful career in the finance organization. How hard could it be to run this business? There were debits and credits, cash flow and capital expenditure, models and systems. How many times had I audited a division, seen the gaping holes in the financials and wondered, "How come you don't get this?"

So here I sit: now I'm the guy that everyone turns to for answers. There is only one problem, the division is a hot mess and I don't know what to do. I'm overwhelmed by the sheer volume of things that consume my day—and very little has to do with the financials.

My typical day is like a retail checkout line on Christmas Eve. I show up by 7am and the early shift lines up at the door. The late shift starts around 2pm and the line lasts until 7pm. That leaves me with the overnight shift to get my own work done. It is lonely at the top, especially on these dark nights. Like quick sand, the more I fight, the deeper I seem to sink.

I would never admit to my boss, my peers, my people or even my close confidents; "I'm stuck and don't know where to turn." My experience at MegaCorp, as I like to call my employer for the past 13 years, is that it is not a place to be vulnerable, to admit you don't know or to ask for help. You're expected to bury your insecurities and your problems.

Sure, everyone *said* just the opposite: "My door is always open for you." "Don't hesitate to ask." "We are a team, here to support each other." But ultimately those that do so are quickly separated from the herd and left to be ravaged by the wolves of economic forces.

That's how I inherited this division. A retiring veteran tossed me this hot potato on his way out the door. Joe was a great guy, everyone liked him. You would ask him, "How's life?" and he would always say, "life's good"—long before that slogan was printed on t-shirts and tire covers. On the surface everything looked hunky-dory. I don't think anyone realized that the arrow was starting to point down.

It took about two months for me to see the hemorrhaging. It was more than the business conditions.

As I walked the hallways, the culture stuck to me like the humidity of an August day in Houston after a thunderstorm. It was oppressive, soaking my shirt in proverbial sweat and making each step incrementally more difficult. It was like everyone in the organization dodged each other, lost in the haze, trying to avoid eye contact and afraid to talk about what was really happening at the company.

So here I sit, eight months in, trying to figure out what to do. Sure my MBA and Finance degrees gave me the tools I needed to clearly see how bad things are right now. I almost wished for ignorance. My education provided models for turnarounds. A nip here, a tuck there, find the strategic levers to pull, seek out new land to farm. The books all made it seem so easy.

All of the textbooks, the case studies, the best practices— they all wrapped things up in nice little bows. I had worked on a case study once during my masters. It was eerily similar to the business where I now served as Executive Vice President. The study was written up in a neat little three-page summary. My thesis, which had garnered an A, was 30 pages.

The only difference between my master's thesis and this real life case study is that this situation can't be summarized in 1,000 pages, never mind three pages. And the solution? That would require a tome rivaling the size of the epic novel *War and Peace*.

Over the past few months I've worked with my leadership team to assess the situation and start working on a plan. Operationally and financially the solution seemed fairly clear. The team carved out a detailed strategy with over

20 unique focus areas and plotted a course. Yet it felt like an invisible boat anchor was dragging on the seafloor anytime we tried to move the bow of the ship.

My brain hurts. Not just from banging my head on the desk, but from trying to untangle this mess. It's like the night my wife dropped all of her tangled necklaces on the table and asked me if I could separate them. The knot of gold, silver and beads still sits on the table at home, just as this snarled mess still sits on my desk.

I lean my chair back and put my feet up on the desk in hopes that some blood will flow back toward my brain. With my hands over my head, I stare at the bookshelf of leadership and management books that I had accumulated over the years. Some I had read front to back, others I had browsed, others I had used as quick reference guides. I will admit, there are many with unturned pages. Some I bought because I liked the pithy title. Others I bought because I wanted to look smart. I always intended to scour the other books looking for the unique secrets they offered.

There are two themes to the books. The first is what I call color-by-number books. They have titles like 6 of these, 10 of those, 15 best practices, 100 most powerful _____, 45 rules of _____, 5 features of _____.

Once I added up all the numbers; they totaled 832 "somethings." Great ideas, all hard to remember, none of which gave me the answers I needed at any given moment. At times it caused me to flit from idea to idea like a squirrel with serious attention deficit disorder all jacked up on mountain dew.

The other theme is the "gods of business" books. These are the leaders, icons and titans we all quote or name-drop at cocktail parties, as if we know them personally and have deciphered all of their secrets. It seemed that these pioneers of business success had some secret answer; otherwise there wouldn't be a book. Their books are easy to recognize because of the names embossed in the title.

I gave up reading these years ago. Many seemed so self-promoting it cast Narcissus into the realm of bashful wallflower. At a glance, it seemed as though these sages could figure out anything, including how to untangle my wife's jewelry jumble. But what I heard from those who've worked around these titans bothered me. There were stories of suppliers being driven to bankruptcy, public firings, people driven to sleep-deprived madness, ruined marriages, and humiliations in large groups. There were also whispers of moral failings in their personal lives. Would I have to become someone I didn't respect in order to grab the brass ring?

Are there authors, leaders, academics and thought leaders who have figured it out?

Yet somewhere on the shelf there had to be an answer, something I was missing that would provide guidance to my current dilemma. I will admit, that as a finance guy by education, some of these ideas seemed a bit soft, hard to quantify and harder to apply. Like trying to grab vapor. Many times the books used words like trust, accountability, influence and motivation. Great words in theory, but vast, complex and difficult in application. I have seen leaders wield these words like weapons, striking down brave corporate soldiers.

I wanted an answer on how to lead this business; something calculable, something quantifiable, something predictable. No more catch phrases, no more cute axioms, no more flavor of the day programs.

So here I sit in my corporate cave pondering how to untangle this mess. I am about to begin another round of forehead pounding when footsteps alert me to someone approaching. The squeak of a wheel tells me it is someone on the cleaning crew. As I put my feet down so it looks like I am actually doing something, a middle-aged woman with a bouncy step, a smiling disposition and an air of confidence enters the office. A baseball hat is on her brow and a ponytail bouncing from the back. I've seen her before, but we have never spoken. She apologizes for interrupting as she grabs the wastebasket from the side of my desk.

As she returns from disposing of another day's worth of meaningless charts, reports and presentations, I decide to engage her. "I have seen you here before, what's your name?"

"Carolyn," she answers.

"How long have you worked for the company?" I ask, assuming that she works for me.

"Oh I don't work for you, my company is contracted to provide facility services for your company."

As if sensing my initial haughtiness she smiles and adds, "It's a lot more complex than it looks."

Wanting to procrastinate and avoid returning to my head banging, I continue my query if for no other reason than to have a conversation with another human being that has nothing to do with work. It is the same reason I occasionally watch mindless sitcoms, letting shows wash over me without needing to think.

"Well, I have to tell you that I appreciate your work, the offices are always in good order. How long have you been doing this?"

"About 15 years."

Surprised that someone would want to do something I considered menial for 15 years, I asked her how she liked it.

"I enjoy it, I like seeing things clean, and orderly. I like the flexibility and I love my clients."

Her use of the term "her clients," as though she is an investment banker, surprises me. After a bit of idle chatter I learn that she actually owns the business. In just over 15 years she had built the company from one person to over 200 people working at a variety of companies in the metro area. It wasn't just cleaning, but other services like office supplies, maintenance, and even some safety training.

Having seen others from her company working in our building, I realize that they also carried an air similar to Carolyn: light hearted, friendly, and committed. She clearly modeled the professionalism and attitude that she wanted her clients to see. Hearing her story of success and reflecting on the quality of her people, it made me realize that yet another person had "a secret" that I don't have.

I ask her how she ended up starting a cleaning business. "I was laid off from this company 15 years ago."

I sit forward rather abruptly at my shock, and I think it scared her. I start looking around the office to see if there are any timers and wires that might have been planted as a form of retribution.

As if reading my mind, she says: "I actually like coming here and keeping tabs on a business I used to work for. I didn't have any hard feelings because if I hadn't been laid off, I would never have been able to pursue this."

I sit back a little more relaxed. "It sounds as though you have had some great success."

"I do feel fortunate but I have had my share of challenges."

"What's your secret?"

"What's your secret?"

She chuckles a bit. "Secret, eh?"

"Well everyone has a secret, and there are 'secrets to success.' There's even a book on the shelf behind you called *The 20 Secrets to Success.*" She turns and admires the bookshelf. In the dim light from my desk lamp the myriad of fonts, colors and graphics gracing the book spines mesh together, forming an impressive visual tapestry against the drably painted office wall.

"I am not sure I have a secret. I am just trying to figure it out every day. When I first started my business I read a lot of these books from business leaders and academics.

I couldn't find a secret. It's not that they didn't have ideas, ways to challenge my thinking and tools I could use. What I needed was a way to apply what I read toward my goals in a more systematic way. I would devour one book, go try to follow someone's model, read the next one and then go follow that idea. Unfortunately, I found I was flitting around."

Well that sounded familiar.

She reaches for one the books and her half sleeve exposes a tattoo on the inside of her right forearm. "I read this book, I really enjoyed the story." She sits down to flip through some pages and I keep looking at her forearm, trying to figure out what could have been worthy of a tattoo. She notices me staring and rolls her hand over to reveal the ink.

"Do you mind me asking what that says?"

She blushes a little. "Oh, it was one of those things you do in college that stays with you. It says $E=MC^2$." I finish her sentence as she says, "Einstein's theory of relativity."

I knew the equation, but what was it doing on our cleaning person, I mean facility services person, I mean business owner. And who goes on a bender in college and decides to get a tattoo of the theory of relativity?

She explains she was a physics student in college. Actually she'd worked in the laser laboratory of our company before the bloodletting 15 years ago that propelled her into her business. This lady was full of surprises.

She tells the usual cliché story, that after a few libations she and her classmates strolled into the local tattoo studio and dared each other to get inked. Of course many of her friends chose the usual designs—tattoos of Bart Simpson, famous quotes, musical notes and drawings that incorporated bodily features. The funniest was someone who had lost a toe in a hunting accident. He instructed them to tattoo an arrow above the stump where there used to be a toe and scribe the words "Gone to market."

She explained that she wanted something that would have meaning for her for a long time. It also had to be simple and elegant. Too many colors and she would have to worry about clashing with clothes she might be wearing. Also it had to be of a style and in a location where it wouldn't morph into an alien or dismembered animal as she aged.

The theory of relativity fit the bill. So I ask her to tell me more about that.

"Einstein developed the equation as a way to understand how the universe works," Carolyn explains. "In this simple equation he created something that we are still unpacking today. It has been used to try to understand time travel, nuclear power and black holes."

Having this reminds me every day that we are all just trying to figure things out, that we need a simple way to distill the complex and something that allows us to continue to deepen our thinking. It's about understanding the relationships between variables that create an outcome.

"He didn't have the answer, but he created a way to pursue the answer and to have deeper understanding of the universe. Having this reminds me every day that we are all just trying to figure things out, that we need a simple way to distill the complex and something that allows us to continue to deepen our thinking. It's about understanding the relationships between variables that create an outcome.

"So," she says, tapping the ink, "this reminds me to keep asking, 'What am I solving for?'"

"Well as much as I would like to continue our conversation, I should let you get back to work and I should finish my rounds."

She says "Night, Jeff," as I bid her a good night as well. Then I wonder, how did she know my name? She didn't ask, and I didn't tell her. It takes me a few minutes in my late night fog to remember that my name is actually on the door. That tells me that it is time to go home. As I leave the office, I grab a marker and write on my whiteboard $E=MC^2$. I am not sure why.

I turn off the desk lamp and head out into a moonless night.

Chapter *2*
R = Impactful Results

When my feet hit the floor this morning, the first thing on my mind is what Carolyn said the night before: "What are we solving for?" The question had been bouncing around in my head as I slept and it occupied my mind as I showered off yesterday's haze and dressed in my fresh corporate uniform for the day ahead.

On the way into the office during the twilight hours of a winter morning, I realize I need time to think about Carolyn's question while I'm fresh. This seems more important than

> **!**
> **What are we solving for?**

whatever emergency would be waiting in line at my office door today. Customer problems, production issues, staffing gaps and technical challenges. The names changed, but the stories were always the same.

Instead of letting the deluge of the morning petitioners pour into my office, I sweep my doorstep clean and let everyone know that I am not available right now. I tell my admin, Sandra, to protect my door as I close it behind me.

I stare at the equation I'd written on my whiteboard the night before. $E=MC^2$. I wonder what I'm solving for and all of the things that we, as an organization, have to solve for. I start scribbling words on the whiteboard. Some are quantitative, such as "profit," "revenue" and "growth."

But many of them are in that list of softer skills like "alignment," "engagement," "ideation" and "trust." Many of the words I'm scribbling are in the titles of the paint-by-number leadership books on my shelf.

Flicking my eyes from the bookshelf back to the whiteboard I settle into my high back chair in my usual position; feet crossed on the corner of my desk, hands crossed on the top of my head. My boss's pronouncement echoes in my mind: "Your job is to lead the organization." I stroll back to the board and write "leadership" near the top.

"Yeah, that doesn't help," I mutter to myself.

"Leadership" is another of those amorphous words that sounds great, but doesn't help me fight the battle I face now. It feels as though I have this label of leader just so that I can be the wring-able neck whenever anyone has a problem.

I know leadership has many characteristics that I need to demonstrate, such as setting a vision, communicating direction, and inspiring people. Every day I put on my leadership cloak embroidered with all these words.

Underneath the cloak lurks the shadow of uncertainty that I hope no one notices. Why do I have to do this alone? Why don't other people put their hands on the oar and help row the leadership boat?

Carolyn's words about the theory of relativity stick with me. Simple elegance, a way to drive deeper meaning. But that question, "what am I solving for?" keeps reverberating.

Then, like a flash, it hits me. RESULTS. At the end of the day we are solving for results, each and every person in the organization. Some are quantitative like sales and profit, some are qualitative like generating new product ideas and developing leadership skills.

I erase all of the words I'd written earlier and write *"Results"* on the upper left hand corner of the board. I don't want all of the other words to distract me or cloud me or cause me to overcomplicate this. I think to myself, "Leadership is ultimately about results."

Leadership is ultimately about results. By now an hour has passed, and it is time to run the proverbial office gauntlet. I garner my armor and sword, bracing for the onslaught every leader can expect when they walk through the building and get ready to slay dragons.

Before I leave, I look at the word *"Results"* one last time and add an equals sign. So it now reads

Results =

— ∞ —

I return to my office after my run through the building, tired, sweaty and bloody. I find the line of petitioners forming at my door like the line at the deli counter. Everyone has a numbered ticket; the next customer sign lights up and people start filing in. Each person comes in with his or her requests, confessions, indictments, appeals, and requisitions.

I am distracted and honestly only half listening. I don't have the energy to dispense my usual sage advice, or so I thought it was sage advice. These sessions have always felt like "vending machine management." Drop a coin in the slot, press a button and advice pops out.

Today, I don't have it in me. I keep glancing at the word "Results." Something was still missing. I think of my homilies about the business results I'd harped on in the past; cut costs, drive revenue, turn cash, get product out the door. I could preach a pretty good sermon from the business bibles.

Yet all of the verses suddenly rang hollow. Then I realize that my homilies had probably rung hollow for my parishioners as well.

The line finally dissipates after a full day of petitions. The sun sets, the offices slowly darken and I find myself alone again, ready to take on the night shift and get my own work done. I'm still drawn to the whiteboard, periodically glancing up from my reports, financials and presentations to look at what I had written.

Once I clear the work pile, I kick back and assume my thinking pose; feet on the corner of the desk, hands on my head. This time when I hear the wheels of the cleaning cart I don't snap forward and pretend to look busy.

Carolyn walks in with a cheery hello. She grabs the trashcan and takes notice of my position. "Taking a little break?"

"Yeah, I am not sure there are many brain cells firing right now." She looks at the whiteboard as she leaves, but has the respect not to ask. She returns with the empty basket and starts to leave to continue her rounds. I ask her if she has a minute and if she would like a bottle of water from the mini-fridge.

"I guess so," she smiles as she humors herself. "As long as you don't tell my boss."

"Let me ask you, what results do you focus on for your business?"

She doesn't even need to think about it before answering. "When I first started out," she begins, "I looked at my typical measurements like revenues, number of proposals, profits, things like that. It worked and it helped, but I started wondering, 'why am I doing this?'"

"It felt like I was working for the bank to pay loans, the government to pay taxes and the insurance companies to pay premiums. Even though everyone said how lucky I was to work for myself, I didn't feel like I was working for me."

I could relate. It seemed as though I was working for everyone else; shareholders, management, financial bean counters, even my own people. I didn't feel like I was working for me.

"So what did you do?"

"Why am I doing this work?"

"I think asking myself the question was far more important than the answer."

She says, "I kept asking myself, 'why am I doing this?' It came to me over time but honestly, I still think about it every day."

Before I can ask what she came up with, she takes the last pull from her water bottle and says, "Well, back to work before the boss catches me slacking." She smiles and bounces off to finish her rounds.

As she leaves my office she pauses and says, "I think asking myself the question was far more important than the answer."

I look at the whiteboard and only feel empty after hearing Carolyn's enigmatic response. I don't have any more clarity about what we are solving for and how to move past the superficial nature of results. It is time to go home and grovel to my wife for being late, yet again. Megan is patient and understanding, but she deserves better. Maybe tonight I will untangle the necklaces as a form of penance.

I turn off the light and head into the darkness of the winter solstice.

The alarm startles me awake at "O" dark hundred hours. Ironically Dave Mathews' song, "Ants Marching," plays on the radio alarm. It makes me want to put my foot down and climb off the merry-go-round. But work we must, and off I march to work. Like the song, I am just an ant marching.

I am the first one in today, like most days. I turn on the light, hang up my coat, wrap my hands around my coffee cup and start thinking about what catastrophes await me today.

I glance at the whiteboard and a flash hits me. "Results are fleeting." We hit our numbers, reach our metrics—yet by the next month, the next quarter, the next year we start over and it is all ancient history. Lost to the ether of time.

It reminds me of those moments when you hit your goals, they magically get increased; rather than letting you celebrate, people ask, "But what are you going to do for me now?" I feel like a circus dog performing tricks for an ever increasingly demanding audience. I write, "Results are fleeting," above the word "Results."

I sit back in my chair and continue to stare, not sure what do with the start of my equation.

Sandra, my admin, arrives and spots me in my thinking pose. She says "morning," lightly and closes the door, somehow knowing I need time to think. An amazing person to work with, Sandra can divine when I need space.

If results are fleeting, why do I care? It seems empty now.

My attention is pulled to another object that I'd carefully pinned beside my desk: a painting that my young daughter made for me. On a sheet of bright red construction paper she'd outlined her hand in various colors. Why did she do that? I know she likes to be creative, and she likes to give her father things for his

> *Results are fleeting:*
>
> *We hit our numbers, reach our metrics—yet by the next month, the next quarter, the next year we start over and it is all ancient history. Lost to the ether of time.*

office. And she always glows when she sees her artwork pinned up near my desk.

The outline of her hand was more than just artwork for her. It reminded me of a trip to Australia where I saw Aboriginal hand paintings in a cave dating back 4,000 years. These prehistoric people would take berries and chew them, hold their hand against the walls and spray the mixture against their hands to create a shadow or outline on the cave wall.

Take away the gross factor of regurgitated food, and there was something in these primal paintings.

Why would they do that? They didn't do it for me so that I could see it 4,000 years later on a vacation. Maybe they did it so there would be some visible demonstration that they had been on this planet. That others would remember them by something that would last longer than their short lifetime on this planet.

That's why we do it; we all want to leave a mark. I go over to the whiteboard and write "*Impact*." After a while, my sentence becomes complete in my mind:

!

Results are fleeting: Impact is lasting.

"Results are fleeting; Impact is lasting."

We all want to leave an impact. That is the answer. I add a word to the equation:

$$Impactful\ Results =$$

That's what we are solving for.

Before venturing out for the day, I scroll through my online pictures and find one I had taken of the aboriginal hand paintings and print it out. I tape it on the whiteboard near the equation. It seems to fit.

It is time to run my daily gauntlet through the office. I refill my coffee, don my armor and head out the door.

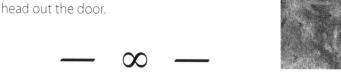

When I return to my office, the line of petitioners has gathered at my doorstep. I take my seat and begin the airing of grievances.

Joe, my head of production, is in front of me complaining about how corporate IT has short-staffed the project we need to get back on schedule.

Joe is one of those tried and true engineers. Very confident and competent. Known for getting things done. He is a bit thinner than the rest of us. I think it is because he is always running somewhere and doesn't get to enough meetings where the infamous corporate cookies are served. He walks with a little bit of a hunch, like he has been carrying the burden of a sack of rocks for a little too long.

I listen to the thread of conversations and emails that Joe assures me have not put a dent in the heavily fortressed corporate stonewall.

Like yesterday, my eyes stray back to the whiteboard as he speaks. I look at the quote. Results are fleeting. Impact is lasting. That seems all fine and good, but how does that help us with this problem, or with any challenge we face?

Then a voice speaks from inside me. I'm not sure from where.

I ask Joe: "Joe, what impact do you want to create here?"

"What impact do you want to create here?"

Joe is stunned, and honestly so am I. At first the wary flash in his eye suggests that he thinks this is a set up, something that is going to get him fired.

Then he looks at my coffee cup and I see him wonder if Sandra spiked my coffee today.

"Let's pause for a minute," I say, trying to keep him steady, bring him back from panic and wild speculation. "Forget about the corporate stonewalling. Let's talk about the impact you want to create."

Joe's eyes spin around like a top trying to process what I just said. Eventually he seems to relax and says, "We need to produce zero defects in a timely fashion for our customers."

I repeat the question with the emphasis on *you*. "Forget about the corporate metrics, what impact do *you* want to create?"

His eyes spin again like the dials on a slot machine until they come to a stop, the buzzer rings and jackpot: "What I really want is to build a production system I am proud of, that showcases our team as leaders in the company."

We don't have an opportunity to pursue the question further because I hear the next customer bell ring and

Sandra informs me I have a meeting. Joe and I hadn't reached any conclusions—but somehow he walks out a little more upright, as though some of the weight of the corporate stonewall has dissipated.

At the end of the day, I am back in the corporate man cave I call my office pondering the day's events. The question I'd put to Joe about impact continues to reverberate through my head. I even asked it a few times in meetings—with surprising results.

Some people shared an inspiring purpose they wanted to fulfill in their work and a desire to accomplish something.

I want to make sure my financials help us make the best decisions for the company and our people.

I want to help serve leaders who want to lead better.

I want our customers to use our products in a way that that enriches their lives.

I was even surprised by people mentioning that they wanted to be challenged to get out of their comfort zone.

I want to grow to be known as a knowledge expert in my area.

I want myself and my team to stretch and embrace the changes we face.

I started seeing handprints all over the place, like the refrigerator door in a house full of toddlers. Except unlike toddler shenanigans, their answers didn't seem messy or annoying at all.

People wanted to leave an imprint. Under their words, I spotted something: pride. In earnestly telling me how they wanted to make an impact, people glowed like parents in the presence of their children. Like I feel when I look at my daughter's hand paintings. They wanted to make an impact, and the responsibility of making an impact lifted them rather than weighed them down.

Of course there were many more who also wondered if Sandra had spiked my coffee.

But I did start to see wheels starting to turn. There was something in the question and in the answers.

Like most leaders, I didn't practice what I preached. I hadn't really asked myself the question nor answered it for myself. What impact did I want to create?

In the silence of the office I assume my thinking pose and stare at the whiteboard, asking myself what impact I wanted to have. I had two problems. First, I had way too many things on my list, and second, I was using general words that sounded like the Boy Scout oath: To honor, obey, be thrifty, to help others.

I doodle on a pad with all of these words until I can't take it anymore. I put it down and sit forward as Carolyn walks in. I didn't hear her wheels rolling down the hallway today and I am a little startled.

"What are you doing here?" she asks.

I start to ramble a response: "Honestly I have no idea. Why are any of us here? What purpose are we serving, does any of this have any meaning in the grand scheme of things?"

After a couple of minutes of babbling, I see in her eyes that she was asking why was I working late, not the existential question about our being.

> **When we are trying to define our impact sometimes our list is too big and it can be too general.**
> **How can we make it very specific and very focused?**

Without being asked she sits down across the desk from me and starts talking to me like a close friend. She listens without judgment as I ramble on about my life-meaning crisis. To my surprise, though we've only spoken briefly a few times, it's easy to open up to her. She interjects some questions as I speak to prompt me along.

"In all of your work, even when you were younger, what really motivated you? What is most important to you right now? What do you want people to say about you long after you have moved on from this assignment? What does this position give you the opportunity to impact?"

After a while she notices I've clearly burned a few neurons and am losing energy fast. "I'm sorry, I probably overloaded you," she says. "These are the questions I am always asking myself. I am sure it feels overwhelming. I believe that when we get more clarity around these questions, we're better able to help our teams get more clarity.

"Don't worry about having the perfect answer, think about what ideas and images it spurs in your mind. When we do this, we get clearer as time goes by. I know you need to get home to your family and I have to get back to my rounds before the boss catches me."

I laugh and thank her for her time. She's right—I don't have the perfect answer yet, but by just the exercise of talking these things over with her, I feel clearer.

In the doorway she adds, "I want to let you know that I appreciate these conversations. I hope I help you, and know that when we talk about these things it helps me get clarity for myself." She bids me good night as I do the same and she bounces out of the office.

After she exits I sit there in my haze a little while longer. My eyes shoot around the room, looking at the quote and equation on the whiteboard, the picture of the primitive hand prints, the paint-by-numbers management books. As my eyes settle on my daughter's hand painting I realize that if I leave now, I will have time to read to her and my son before they go to bed.

How can you have a bad day when you return home and receive the eager greeting of your children and have a chance to read to them on your lap while their breath warms you like a mid-summer sun? I have to make more time for this.

After I put my son and daughter to bed, my wife and I settle down with a glass of wine to share our days' adventures.

I listen as Megan shares the events of her day. Getting our kids to school, working on homework projects, volunteering at the school and supporting the charity she is so passionate about. I think many people perceive stay-at-home moms to be a break from reality.

As Megan talks, I realize she has no breaks. It is a non-stop day for her too. However, instead of being wrung out like an old dishrag, she seems to glow. A tired glow, but a glow nonetheless, like the afterglow of a good workout.

Even though Megan had a career of her own prior to our children, she seems so motivated by what she is doing now. I envy her. Her purpose is far more meaningful than mine: "making the world safe for MegaCorp products."

As I share my day I nervously venture into to my cloudy thinking around the equation and the quote, certain that she'll find my thoughts more than a little flaky. She doesn't though. She reinforces my thoughts around the word impact.

She says, "What I always admired about you in your college activities, your jobs, your volunteer work, even helping the neighbors is that you always strive to leave an impact. I think that is a good word for you."

"So," she asks. "What impact do you want to have?" The question hits with the dull thud of a grapefruit hurled at a brick wall. I have no idea.

What impact do you want to have?

After some disorganized discussion of the ideas floating from my head to my mouth, I realize that

I am not going to make sense of this tonight. We have exhausted the conversation, our glasses of wine and we are both exhausted. It is time to crash.

The alarm clock goes off and I wake up with that feeling that I had the weirdest dream. It left me with that unsettled feeling that I knew would hang with me for the day. I hit the snooze and lay there trying to remember the dream.

I had died, and was drifting in the afterlife.

Note to self: No more wine before bed.

I drifted past all of the people I had known in my life. They were family members, teachers, mentors, pastors and coworkers. Each greeting me warmly. As each person touched me, I felt something pass into me. Like a pulse of energy.

Seriously, no more wine before bed.

I'm still foggy when the alarm sounds again, time to get up. As I shower, dress and drive to work I keep trying to hold onto the vapor of the dream while simultaneously trying to discard it as some kind of alcohol-induced fantasy.

When I arrive at the office, Joe is first in the requisitions line. He is back to talk about the corporate stonewalling, only it is different today.

He admits that my question yesterday about "his impact" made him wonder if I had taken a proverbial trip back to Woodstock. But then he told me that the question prompted a whole different conversation with his team about the problems they faced. The conversation managed to move past the personality conflicts and barking at the moon about corporate issues.

Instead, they defined the impact they wanted to have as a team. They even wrote it down. It was similar to what Joe had said earlier, only what they came up with seemed to have the handprints of the entire team stamped into it.

I feel this pulse of energy from Joe; somehow I had impacted him in a way I didn't even recognize.

In turn, Joe impacted me because I see that what he had done with his own team could be replicated for the leadership team. I ask Sandra to clear my schedule for the morning and bring the leadership team together.

Joe regrets sharing what he came up with because now I'm asking him to lead the discussion among our leadership team about the same thing for the entire division. I'm sure he sees it like those times you raise your hand with an idea and you walk out of a meeting with action items.

Sensing his fear of "what did I just get signed up for"? I let him know that all I want him to do is lead a conversation with the leadership team to get people talking. By sharing his experience it will spur the teams along. I see the relief on his face, and he heads out to organize a time for everyone to come together.

The leadership team, Joe, and I spend the morning hashing out the different perspectives. Obviously finance wants to have a different impact than human resources and operations.

Rather than try to write it by committee, the team chooses one person to generate a draft that distills everything we've discussed. More importantly, each member of the team noted that they wanted to do the same exercise with their respective teams. I see another big pulse of energy among the team and I see the impact spreading through the organization.

It was a good discussion, but it still didn't feel like it was helping us with our challenges of the day. So I don my armor and head out to slay dragons for the day, guessing that it will be more rewarding than a mental exercise. Yet I know there is something important to be solved for with the team.

When I return to the office I find the impact statement for the team on my whiteboard in glowing orange letters. It declares: "We impact the lives of our customers by providing leading-edge products, we impact ourselves by challenging each other to grow and we impact our people by providing rewarding and sustainable work that fills their purpose."

Underneath it says, as if to qualify the impact statement: "If we achieve this impact, we will meet our business metrics."

A disclaimer below says: *This is a first draft only and subject to continued revision based on the input of others and changes in business conditions.*

Somehow I know legal must have had a hand in this.

The day is winding down and I dismiss the remaining petitioners, close the door and start to think. I appreciate the qualifying point about business metrics because the old finance mantra, "Cash is King," reverberates in my head. So how does this connect to our impact statement?

Thinking of the previous owner, I realize that if we deliver the cash and leave dead bodies spread around the building, it won't sustain us. I go over the whiteboard again and modify the saying—"Cash is King, Culture Trumps All."

Just then, like clockwork, Carolyn walks in. She greets me and heads for the bins. Today she has some kind of electronic gadget with a wand. She waves it around as she passes through the office. I am hoping she is spreading good karma. Disappointingly, it's a device used to measure air quality, something Carolyn's business does for my company and for her other clients.

Cash is King, Culture Trumps All.

I wonder what she might have picked up in the air after our discussion about impact.

I ask if her boss would let her join me for a few minutes. As I go to get her a water bottle from my mini-fridge, she notices the new writing on the board. She asks me how I came up with all of that. I explain that the team came up with the impact statement—to which she asks: "How is that different than a vision statement?"

"Good question." I start thinking out loud and share my frustration that too many vision statements seem to be pabulum; lacking meaning, relegated to fancy print on foam boards, but not connected to the people of the company. My last company had a vision statement full of twenty-five-cent words strung together that didn't add up to more than a nickel." She chuckles.

In a stream of consciousness I say, "I hope that each person finds a place to leave their impact, and that by defining it as an 'Impact Statement' that it may be more meaningful to everyone. It might even open the door for each group and even each individual to create their own impact statement. It is my hope that they have a deeper connection between what the company does, what they do in their job and their own personal purpose."

"What about that quote about cash?" Carolyn asks.

I explain that I am trying to move beyond business results and it just came to me.

She presses on: "But why culture, in particular—how does that relate to cash?"

I explain that culture is simple: it is what we talk about and how we talk about it. Amazed at my own little flash of brilliance I go write it on the board: "Culture is what we talk about and how we talk about it."

"So how does that relate to solving for results here?"

I ponder the question, and after some back and forth I say, "Without a strong culture, we can't replicate the cash we are generating, thus the results become fleeting."

"Sounds cool, I think you are on to something." Carolyn shares a story from back when she still worked for the laser laboratory of our company.

When the company was acquired it had a very toxic culture. It was every man and woman for themselves. People didn't talk about the real needs of the business (such as building a strong product pipeline) and no one seemed to care. The firm that acquired us constantly harped on cash generation. What happened was a very quick failure and within a short period of time. That's why the business had a bloodletting 15 years ago. Ultimately they sold this division to MegaCorp at a substantial loss.

> **!**
>
> **Culture is what we talk about and how we talk about it. Without a strong culture, we can't replicate the cash we are generating, thus the results become fleeting.**

As she finishes her story, she gets up and starts to prepare to go back to her rounds. "Nice work on that," Carolyn says. She nods approvingly at the newest additions to the whiteboard. "Thank you for sharing it with me. I think I should do the same for my business if you don't mind me learning from your work."

"Of course," I say, knowing that imitation is flattery.

She gathers her wand and finishes her water as she heads out to continue her collection of papers and air quality samples.

I continue to ponder the history and impact of the business. The impact created by the founder, Hans Large, continues to this day, even though he has long since passed. The business was founded to launch a new technology in the 1930s.

Although the original technology is obsolete, the products built off the original invention continue to be used today. You can see the fingerprints and handprints, not only from Hans and the company he founded, but from the myriad of other companies that spawned from the original research started here. It is amazing to see this even after it has been sold, acquired, divested, integrated and any other number of iterations.

I saw the founder speak once years ago. When I reflect on his talk I realize that he was someone who truly wanted to change the world. One of the things that he said really stuck with me: "We hope that the imprint of our companies' technologies can be seen in the quality of lives around the world." He also talked about creating a place where others could come to leave their impact.

It is about creating a place where others can come to leave an impact.

That's why, in its heyday, the company attracted some great scientists. Even beyond the technology, there were people from this company that were recognized for marketing innovation and customer service. It seems like *that* impact was more important than creating "cash" or "building a bigger business."

I realize that my being here is bigger than the business metrics; it's about creating a culture that I was proud of, about doing work I found important, and leaving an impact beyond the daily dragon slaying.

I make a note to myself to think about "my" impact. For now, I think the team has a great start at a strong impact statement for our leadership team. This is the beginning of creating something bigger than our quarterly results.

I grab my coat to head out the door, and on my way I stop to look at the beginning of my equation "Impactful Results =" and review the leadership group's impact statement: "We impact the lives of our customers by providing leading-edge products, we impact ourselves by challenging each other to grow, and we impact our people by providing rewarding and sustainable work that fills their purpose."

My head feels drained, and I head home, fully spent as though I've had a hard day of training at the gym. I need to get off this treadmill of 13-hour days before my saintly wife takes me to task for another late night at the office. Fact is, this isn't a sustainable pace for the long term. If I keep it up, the only impact I'll have is the sound my body makes as it hits the floor when I drop dead in my office.

Megan and I sit down after the kids go to bed to debrief the day. She shares all the travels and trials with the kids and tells me about her meeting with one of her community involvements. I'm envious of the number of places where she impacts others. I am especially appreciative of the impact she has on our kids. With her influence I'm confident that they will grow into functioning adults.

I share my evening conversation with Carolyn with her and my reflections about the definition of impactful results as the foundation for my equation. I admit that I am still not clear about how to make the word "Impact," impactful (not to be redundant). On the other hand, I am clear that the word "Results" by itself is lacking something.

I appreciate her asking what impact means to me and why I think the word results is lacking. I share with her the feeling of emptiness every time I have to report "my numbers." Of course there is the benefit of achieving something measurable, but I also know results are short lived. Even when we exceed our numbers, it's forgotten by the next day and I'm back to receiving the "what have you done for me lately?" questions. I can only imagine that my people feel the same about the results they have to report.

"I imagine this cascades all the way through the organization to the people working on the front line," I confide. "I can almost hear the emptiness of our measured results echo through the hallways."

"I can almost hear the emptiness of our measured results echo through the hallways."

Megan gives a knowing nod that comes from her time serving as a corporate soldier, and from working with charitable groups to reach their metrics. "So if results were truly impactful, what would they look like, sound like or feel like to you and others?"

Great question. I start rambling while Megan jots notes onto a pad in her lap. I can't tell what she is writing, but when she catches me trying to peek she pulls it out of my sight. Abandoning my curiosity, I continue on, focusing on verbalizing my thoughts.

So if results were truly impactful, what would they look like, sound like or feel like to you and others?

I share examples of things that I think would represent real impact beyond the numbers. Clearly action with everyone rowing in the same direction on the same things is important. So instead of production working on one thing, and sales another, they would work in concert more effectively to move customers from orders through delivery.

I also talk about the importance of trust because too many times trust, or lack thereof, gets in the way. We have teams that don't trust each other, we have many people who don't trust the corporate office and in some places people don't trust our customers. I heard someone say the other day that "This customer is just trying to milk us for everything we are worth." In too many cases the lack of trust negatively impacts our results.

One of the things that gets in the way of trust is conflict. Now at first I talk how conflict erodes trust. "But you know what, sometimes the lack of conflict erodes trust." People are usually aware when there are challenges and issues. By not addressing them head-on, however, people tend to feel less than authentic (and judge others as less than authentic). Instead they might talk about the conflict to others somewhere in the recesses of the office. I'd done it myself. Afterwards I'd always feel like I needed a shower.

I imagine it has the same impact on the other people in the company. Moreover, when I hear people complain about someone else, knowing they chose not to address it with that person or group, it makes me wonder what they don't say to me. There has to be a way to use conflict to motivate us to action versus running for cover.

Megan nods along as she listens to my soliloquy. I continue rambling.

"There also is a need for a connection between the results we are trying to achieve and each person's goals. Not just the job goals, but even their life goals or why they even show up for work."

It's frustrating when one of my supervisors comments, "Every person gets recognition every two weeks in the form of a paycheck, what else do they want?" The reality is that pay is only a portion of why people show up for work. Pay is important but it only gives us arms-and-legs compliance; it does nothing to captivate their inspiration, their creativity and their hearts.

!

When we connect each person's impact to the organizational impact, we unlock power.

Megan carries on writing notes and even doodling little pictures, something she often does as a way to process and synthesize what she hears. I am now expounding on the connectedness between people. "If we are going to have an impact, we have to recognize that we need to influence others. When we don't work together, or even worse, work against each other, it creates very real damage."

!

If we are going to have an impact, we have to recognize that we need to influence others.

I recall one of our researchers coming into my office to talk about an idea she had come up with, one that she thought was the greatest thing since the invention of the light bulb. However, her idea had been summarily dismissed by others in the company. She was very bright and always had good ideas, but this wasn't the first one to be dismissed out of hand. Maybe not every idea of hers was a winner, but I knew we'd passed over some great ones because people didn't listen.

"After listening to her complaints, yet again, I said something that has stuck with me ever since. I said to her, 'I hear what you are saying. It makes me wonder if it is one of three things: either it wasn't the great idea you just thought it was, it was a great idea and you didn't sell it well enough, or the timing wasn't right."'

I wasn't trying to shut her down, but she did stop in her tracks. By the look in her eyes I knew she was going to ponder her next course of action. I explained to her that many of us had experienced this same thing, and it is a good reminder to make sure we reflect on why our ideas aren't accepted. We need to think about that "selling it" part more often because, outside of the sales team, many of us don't feel we should have to sell or we don't feel comfortable as a salesperson. However, if we can't influence others, we will run the risk of coming up short on new ideas.

> *If you haven't influenced others to accept your idea maybe it is one of three things: It isn't the great idea you just think it is, it's a great idea and you haven't sold it well enough or the timing isn't right.*

I stop babbling to Megan because I realize I have been going on for some time and I am a little out of breath. I sit back to suck in a little oxygen. "I appreciate you listening, but I don't know if I made any sense. Or if it helps me define what impact really means."

"I heard a lot about what it means to you," Megan counters. "And I think it makes sense, it just needs a little organization." She flips over her pad and shows the doodling and words she had written down as I was talking.

Bam, she nailed it in a simple mnemonic. I also like how she drew it in creative characters using her artistic abilities (of which I have none).

She explains that I had touched on each of these words while describing what impact meant to me. "Maybe these six words can be used to prompt the team to think about how they create impact."

I ask her if I can keep the pad, to which she smiles and says of course. This is going in my office next to my whiteboard and the equation. I ask her to sign the bottom so we remember it is a Megan original.

The next day, we use Megan's drawing in our staff meeting to talk about how we can make sure we achieve truly impactful results for ourselves and others. I explain how we can use the mnemonic as a reminder of what creates impact. It is not intended to be in the order of the letters in the word, but to help us think about what parts might move us beyond the superficial metrics to lasting impact.

By explaining what Megan had captured, it helps me get clearer and get the team engaged in driving deeper impact. I explain how the I represents the necessity to use positive influence strategies to engage others and generate new ideas. Without influence, we are stuck working in a vacuum.

Diane, the head of sales, points out that this could cause people to feel we need to be political, "and some employees think we are already too political."

I always like her thinking. Diane is as sharp as the bright colors she wears to accent her business suits. I agree and explain something I remembered from my philosophy class in college. I am paraphrasing and hope I am doing justice to the original text: "Aristotle said politics is nothing more than the vehicle we created when we went from living as nomads, to living in community. It makes sense to me because we are always politicking, negotiating and influencing."

Politics is nothing more than the vehicle we created when we went from living as nomads, to living in community. We are always politicking, negotiating and influencing.

I continue, "I believe there are good politics and bad politics. Bad politics are at the expense of others for selfish reasons; good politics are for the betterment of a greater purpose. That's why I like to talk about positive influence strategies." Based on the body language of the group, I think this helps explain the importance of the **I** for influence in impact.

!

Bad politics are at the expense of others for selfish reasons; good politics are for the betterment of others and for a greater purpose.

M should remind us to look for each person's individual motivators and connect them to the result we are trying to create. Some are motivated by new learning opportunities where others are motivated by having more time with their family. Don't depend on the paycheck alone. By tailoring our recognition to personal motives, we can supercharge the organization.

I continue by sharing what I call "the sin of institutional recognition." This is what we get when we create recognition programs that turn into "whose turn is it to be recognized today?" By adding a personal touch and connecting it a person's purpose, we can truly impact motivation.

!

Avoid the sin of institutional recognition.

The **P** for purpose should help us look deeper and beyond motivators. We each have a purpose. It isn't always clear to us. "We can acknowledge that I have a different purpose than each of you, and each of you have different purposes than your people. If we can connect individual purpose to the results we are trying to create, we can engage people's heads, hearts and souls."

The **A** for action should remind us to focus on those actions that can have the greatest impact. "As a matter of fact," I say as I look around the room at all of our charts, "we need to get better at focusing on the most powerful actions we can drive to create impact."

That's when I bring up the topic of **C** for conflict. I notice the team literally push away from the table, as though they want to avoid any potential conflicts with their whole person. I explain that I don't like conflict either. "But when we see conflict we should recognize a gap. A gap in what we expect and what we experience.

I pause to let the team absorb what I just said and to go write on the white board. On the right side I scribe the word *Expect*, on the left, the word *Experience*. I draw a line between the two words with arrows on both ends of the line.

> *Conflict is a gap between what we expect and what we experience.*

We see conflict as huge gaps and sometimes they are. These huge gaps create huge problems. But sometimes the conflict gap is small. We ignore it, and then the gap widens. If we could start seeing the small gaps when they start, we can avoid the bigger problems later.

Whether it is a small or a large gap, if we learn to see conflict in that way, to name it more effectively and talk about it (versus avoid it) I think we can create great things.

"Honestly, when I look at the **T** for Trust, it reminds me that it is one of those words that I really struggle with. When someone says 'trust me' or 'we need to trust' my first reaction is not to trust. That's because too many times people that use these words are those who have proven they can't be trusted.

"We know we need to trust, but we also have lots of reasons for not trusting. Trust can actually be built when conflict meets robust conversation. The best way for us to build trust is to get better at talking with our people, being transparent when we can be and dealing with conflict when we see it."

Trust can be built when conflict meets robust conversation.

Robert, the head of HR, says, "Like trust, the transparency word bothers me because we can't be transparent. There are always things we can't share. That causes people to distrust us, or the company."

Karen, the head of IT, joins the conversation: "But we can be transparent about transparency." This comment draws a look of confusion.

Be transparent about transparency.

Karen slides her reading glasses up on her head as she elaborates: "I had a boss who would say this about transparency: 'look team, I can't always tell you everything, but if I know and I can share it, I will make every effort to tell you. If I don't know, I will tell you I don't know and try to find an answer. But also recognize there are things I may know something about, but don't have enough information to share it with you. If that is the case, I will make every effort to tell you that I can't comment. I hope you will understand that there are times when there is need for absolute confidentiality.' That took a lot of the guesswork out of what transparency meant."

I think it is because of her background in technology that Karen has this ability to express things succinctly and formulaically so that people get it.

We continue to explore the meaning of each word. Everyone has examples of things they've run into that relates to one of the six letters. All of this talk about the elements of IMPACT shows the team is getting a clearer vision around how they can create deeper impact than just numbers. I am feeling much more complete now that we have a better handle on what impact means for each of us.

I think we are ready to dive into what's on the other side of the equals sign.

Chapter *3*
A = Focused Actions

After another long day in the office full of meetings and fire drills, I find myself in the operations War Room. That's what we call it. It's a conference room we had wallpapered with charts, diagrams and action plans. It is where we meet throughout the day to check in, manage projects, plan, and, like the name of the room said, make our war plan. And what a war it was.

I am in my thinking pose, feet on the table, hands over my head, looking at the walls when Carolyn passes through. She needs a payloader to haul out the pile of papers generated in this room.

"Looks like you found a change of scenery," she says as she hoists the large bin of paper. When she returns she is waving her magic wand. That's the name I have given to her air quality device.

"Should I be worried about breathing this air?" I ask her.

"No, not at all, my engineers are making some changes to the air purification system and we want to make sure it is working."

"And . . ." I say waiting for her report.

"So far so good."

Knowing she is a physicist by trade and that she had worked at the company, I ask her what she makes of all this. I gesture to the four walls peppered with papers.

"Hmm, well, first I am impressed with the volume of activity here, your team has a lot on their plate. Given all of this paper, I wonder 'what is the glue that holds it all together?'"

I know she is not referring to the masking tape holding the papers to the wall. "I was just wondering the same thing. The volume of work and pace of activity is frenetic. Like an ant hill next to an open jar of honey."

Referring back to our conversation about the equation, I joke, "I feel like our biggest impact is on the masking tape and paper businesses."

She chuckles. "I remember learning about $E=MC^2$. We take for granted what the equals sign means, but it is actually a powerful symbol. I liked the description a professor gave me for what the equals sign represents. She said, 'think of the equals sign as a pipeline through which one side of the equation is converted to the other. In this case how energy is converted into mass.'"

"Wow, that's a little mind bending."

"Facility services and mind blowing, that's my business." She smiles as she heads out the door waving her wand.

Left with my thoughts, I wonder, "What is on the other side of that pipe that will be channeled to create impactful results?"

Clearly it is everything on this wall. If I'm honest though, I would admit (and the team would

> *The equals sign is the pipeline through which one side of the equation is converted to the other. What is on the other side of that pipe that will create impactful results?*

admit) that there's more on this wall than we can accomplish with the resources we have.

I start to feel a bit helpless. Does that mean we can't create the results we want? Even more so, with the demands shouting at us from these walls, how can we ever focus on impact? If we're constantly bailing out the boat, we're not spending time sailing.

I walk back to my office and look at the beginning of the equation. *Impactful Results =*. What gets channeled through the pipe of our equals sign?

I go up to the board and write *Actions*.

$$Impactful\ Results = Actions$$

Of course actions create results. Clearly we had enough actions defined. The War Room walls were littered with actions, dare I say, "too many actions."

Something is missing; it has to be more than just action. My phone rings and it's the kids, calling to say goodnight.

Ouch, it can't be that late. I realize I am getting more time with our facilities person than I am with my family. It is time to leave. I turn off the lights and leave our partial equation to slumber in the twilight.

On the way home, I think about how important it is to get this time with my family. The kids aren't going to be kids forever. I remember someone I worked with once told me, "Fully commit to the business and you will never want."

What a self-serving bunch of crap that was. I knew he wasn't going to be there when my kids were in therapy, when my wife left me, when I was lying on the examination table with a dire diagnosis.

At the same time, I want to be successful, I want the business to thrive, I want my people to have an enriching experience. I am overwhelmed by the sheer volume of things I have to do. How do I get to the actions I know are necessary (like time with family, taking care of my health, continuing to learn) so I can continue to be effective at my job and in my life while also achieving these business goals?

Those questions will have to wait until tomorrow.

When I arrive in the morning, I stop by my office long enough to drop my coat, unpack my briefcase and head for the weekly progress review in the War Room. As I leave my office I glance at the equation and feel the emptiness of the word "Actions." There is a nagging discomfort that something is missing. I head to the War Room ready to go to battle.

This four-hour meeting was more like a rugby scrum than an organized battle. Everyone huddles, and then the kicking, biting and scratching starts. I watch the scrum at a distance, scanning the wallpaper and thinking about the emptiness of the word "actions."

Then it hits me like a lightning bolt, and it jolts me so much that I sit forward abruptly and startle the rest of the group. As if it is one continuous motion I stand up and leave the room with a passing, "Gotta go."

I am sure that the scrum will continue after I leave, exactly as it would have if I had stayed in the room.

I return to my office and insert my lightning-bolt word on the whiteboard next to the word Actions: *FOCUSED*.

Impactful Results = Focused Actions

We are lacking focus. The key to solving for impactful results is to have focused actions. Sure, we had every kind of project planning chart, control chart and metric you could think of, but there was a lack of focus. How could we focus, with the sea of wallpaper we'd fastened to the War Room walls? The sheer volume of things we needed to work on would blur any attempt at focus.

Focus can be our glue that holds it all together. I grab a stack of colorful 5x7 index cards and head back. I jump into the middle of the scrum and push my arms out to separate everyone. I have officially hijacked the meeting.

"OK team, go grab a coffee, take a bio break. I want to meet with the leadership team back here in 10 minutes. We are going to change gears."

Joe, my head of production, looks at me sideways, bewildered, probably wondering what was coming and annoyed that I was taking over his meeting.

Those not on the leadership team leave nervously, probably with a fear that heads are about to roll. Fear is the usual reaction anytime the leadership team meets behind a closed door. I reassure those exiting that there are no impending pink slips.

Even though that hasn't happened on my watch, it's the reaction that seems ingrained in the corporate psyche. I go to the whiteboard and write the equation (using the impact statement the leadership team had written), an equals sign, and focused actions.

When the team comes back from their break I tell them I think we need to get some focus if we are going to have the impact they decided they want to have. "So let's talk about the most important things we need to focus on in order to get to the result you defined."

The team jumps in with a flurry of ideas, thoughts and suggestions. It is disorganized, disorderly and disheveled. But it is necessary.

I let it go on and listen; for now I'm not letting the lack of focus worry me. After about an hour, Robert, our head of HR says, "Aren't these the same things we talked about when we created the 20-point plan…" He looks at me as he finishes, "…when you first got here?"

Robert is a very disciplined ex-marine, which is exactly what this division needs in his role. He is always perfectly dressed, pressed and shined. He likes order and I know he had a hand in the 20-point plan.

I smile and nod.

"So what are we doing here, recreating the wheel?"

Diane, our head of sales jumps in and asks Robert, "How many of the 20 key strategies can you name?"

Robert gets to the third one and starts to stumble.

Karen from IT jumps in: "I agree, the list of 20 always felt like too much. We need to narrow it down. I am not surprised that Robert, or any of us for that matter, can name only a few. And we were the ones who created the plan! How much do you think our people remember?"

Robert says, "OK, but how many should we have?"

Karen starts talking about telephone numbers and I wonder where she is going. "In the telephone business, there is a reason why phone numbers are broken into a hyphenated 3-3-4 scheme," she explains. "If I gave you a straight string of 10 numbers, you probably wouldn't be able remember them all. But by breaking the phone number down into two blocks of three and a single block of four digits, our brains retain them better. It seems like we should be able to name the three or four core strategies easily and in an easily remembered way."

I grab my stack of colored cards and deal out four red cards. "Here you go; we have four cards. Let's put our key actions on these four."

After a couple of hours of hashing through the 20-point tome, the wallpaper and the various agendas, the team came up with the four things that can have the most powerful influence on the impactful results they defined. Robert has been scribing everything down and even after all the disorder of reforming our focus, he seems to continue to stand straight. I am glad because if he felt we weren't organized, structured or disciplined he would be the first one to call it out. Everyone seems satisfied, but mentally drained.

"I recommend we break and get back to the business of 'making the donuts,'" I say.

We huddle, yell, "Break!" and head out to our respective positions on the field. I stay behind and neatly transcribe the four items onto clean 5x7 cards; it is a necessity to feed the obsessive compulsive in me. Each of the four has a different color. They are:

- Define a pipeline of 3 products that allows us to leapfrog our competitors.

- Decrease our time to market by half.

- Provide an engaging and impactful experience for all partners. *

- Streamline our production process to make product cheaper, with fewer part numbers and better quality.

*"Partners" is a new word the team came up with to replace employees, manager, and supervisor. The logic is that no one likes to be an employee. The team thought that "partner" set a new context for how everyone works together.

Would you rather be an employee, subordinate, manager, boss or be a partner to others?

I stick them to the wall and head out. It is early afternoon and I realize that it is time to put my foot down and slow the merry-go-round. I call my wife to tell her I am picking the kids up after school and to clear the decks. We spend the evening at the local restaurant by the lake. Through the oversized windows, we watch the townspeople ice skate under the floodlights. The music playing over the sound system seeps into the restaurant, adding to the ambiance.

After dinner, we decide to lace the kids up and give them a push to the ice. While I'm lacing up my son's skates, my daughter tells him, "You have magic skates that will help you learn how to glide smoothly across the ice." She helps her little brother as he stumbles awkwardly onto the ice. She holds his hand and encourages him. He is learning, with his sister's help. Just as she learned from us.

I think to myself, "I need to get me some of those magic skates to wear at work." Then I start to think about how to get magic skates for our production team, R&D, everyone. Realizing that I am being drawn back into the mental work vortex, I turn to engage Megan, to be in the moment with her without letting the dragons of my workday sneak out of the shadows and destroy this moment.

We sit on the bleachers and watch the kids with the inner warmth that is fueled by pride and contentment. The cool night, the hot chocolate, and the sparkle off the misty snowflakes is picturesque. Although the night is dark, the ambient light off the snow seems to illuminate the night as if it were day. That will keep the dragons at bay.

I apologize to my saintly wife for not being home very often. While she's patient and understanding, I know my absence takes a toll. There are times I call her my Mother Theresa, but then I backtrack because that saint is much older than my wife and not the dating type.

That night I sleep with a clarity I haven't had in a while. No restlessness, no waking in the middle of the night thinking about something I need to do the next day. Just sound sleep from the fresh air and the glow of my family.

It lasts. In the morning, I don't feel the same hovering black cloud of urgency waiting to rain down on my day.

I have called the leadership team into the War Room and notice an acronym written on the whiteboard next to the four items they defined the day before: *H.I.P.* I chuckle to myself. I think it is someone trying to be HIP.

As they come into the room, I query as to who wrote it and what it means. Diane turns out to be the author and explains that during the night she wanted to give a name to our defined items. But she wanted to avoid the usual corporate lingo of Goals, Strategies and Objectives. So HIPs mean **H**ighest **I**mpact **P**ursuits.

Robert's not entirely convinced at first: "Don't we need goals and strategies?"

"This can become our lens for defining our goals, strategies and objectives," Diane says. "The pursuits are more about focus."

Highest

Impact

Pursuits

***Pursuits are about strategic focus**

Everyone seems to like the term; it is catchy and different. I put us in motion by saying, "So let's get HIP," and immediately realize how unhip I sound.

Everyone groans and Diane says, "How about we call them HIP pocket items, as in something simple and easy we can pull out of our hip pocket when we are deciding what to work on." OK, that sounds better.

I deal out the index cards, using blue cards to represent defining the product pipeline, purple cards for decreasing the time to market, green cards for engaging all partners, and orange for streamlining production.

But I add one more color. I give them one black card each. First, I ask them to take the color-coded cards and match them up to the activities and actions taped to the wall.

Karen looks at the stack of color cards and the papered walls and with her usual analytic mind does a quick calculation comparing the number of cards and the huge volume of actions, and says, "Hey wait, we don't have enough cards."

She caught me. I had carefully counted out cards to limit the number of items they could tag in each area. "Well," I say, "unfortunately we don't have unlimited resources, so you are going to have to pick which actions are critical to supporting the HIP items and therefore will have the greatest ability to create the impact you want to have."

"What about the black card?" Robert asks.

"Ahh, yes. First, you will have items that don't get a colored card. That's OK, there will be things that are not directly aligned but are still necessary. But it is important we lighten the load. So if there is something that doesn't fit and you want to get rid of it, give it a black card."

I start to head out the door and Diane asks me, "Where are you going? Aren't you going to join us?" She, like everyone else, assumes I am going to play the usual role of arbitrator reigning over all the decisions in my kingdom.

But I realized last night: it was time for me to let go. I can't control everything. There are a few key things I need to do to have an impact. Giving the leadership team room to figure things out is one of them. Besides, they're smart; there's not much I'm going to add to this level of detail.

I head back to my office and return the usual corporate calls asking for information, updates and decisions. As I take the calls, I keep glancing up at the equation.

$$Impactful\ Results = Focused\ Actions$$

I start to squirm because I realize it is still missing something (or somethings) and I have no idea what. I spend most of my day in the office processing the pile of corporate paper that keeps coming my way. It's necessary, but so are taxes, it doesn't mean I have to like it. Also, like taxes, one department or another was always making new requests, new demands, and new processes. Just like taxes, they always add more, no one ever takes away.

I decide that I need to do a little organizing of my own, and start sorting all the paper into the same four HIP categories. I add one that is non-negotiable. There are things that have to be done that can't be overlooked. For example, compliance, legal and safety.

When I was done, I had five manageable piles and a huge pile with all the items that didn't fit. I take the leftovers and put them on my credenza. I figure if someone really needs it they will call to ask about it. I could have a conversation to see how critical the task really is, and if there was a better way to attend to it. Anything that didn't merit a phone call could just accumulate for now.

I finish my stacks in record time. Looking at the remaining pile, I say to myself, "No wonder I am always here late." That pile was costing me an extra five hours per week.

I head back to the War Room at the end of the day to see how the team has done. The room has a whole different feel.

That pile was costing me an extra five hours per week.

First, it is a heck of a lot more colorful. All the colored note cards add some brightness to the room. But also, one of the walls is now blank, with nothing stuck to it. I am shocked, there are actually walls and windows behind all the taped up papers. I had forgotten that the conference room even had windows to the outside world.

The team also has a different feel. They are more energized and seemingly unburdened. They walk me through their conversations and what they came up with. Although it took some real horse-trading, they removed a volume of things that didn't support their HIP focus.

The leftovers are neatly stacked in the corner. The pile has a note: "Discard after June 1st," a date a few months away in case they needed something. I make a note to myself to put a similar note on the pile on my credenza.

It feels as though a huge weight had been lifted from this room. The team had made great progress, but there was more to do. For example, communicate the four HIPs to the rest of the teams and involve them in the sorting process.

Robert adds some hard work the leadership team might need to do. "I think our teams believe that every time something comes up, or we mention something, that it has to be put on a list or someone's action items. That's how these walls got so thick with paper."

I confess to myself that I have added to the layers on the wall. I am famous for walking down the hallway and musing over an idea out loud. By the time I get to my office it has already shown up on someone's action plan.

Robert continues, "If we keep a disciplined focus on this, we can also show the team how this will help them decide what is really important in order to reach our end game."

Peter, our contemplative head of R&D in the corner adds in: "If we do that, though, I think we should expect some pushback from others when we toss out an idea."

"Heck, we should encourage them to do so," says Karen.

I pull out my pulpit to preach for a few minutes before we break. "I agree, we need to encourage good discord. Just be mindful that we, as a leadership team, can be the ones that limit people's willingness to do so."

Everyone takes on an expression of "Who, me?"

I continue: "It isn't intentional. There are times when someone raises something and we push back, defend or discount. Although we think we are just processing the idea, our people can take it as being shut down."

As a wrap-up I add, "I only suggest that we keep a mindful eye on how we communicate our actions and how it impacts the people around us, that's all."

Everyone agrees and heads out with a clearer mind on our focus and thinking about how to leverage that with our partners.

Chapter 4

I = Interrelationships

Carolyn walks in as I am pondering the War Room walls and the equation. I think that she senses my uneasiness, that I am missing something.

"Hey, someone did some redecorating here."

I explain to her what the team was working on, the HIP items, the sorting and the cleaning out of the unnecessary.

"A little spring cleaning is always a good thing," she says.

With pride, I let her know that I think the team has solved for the FOCUSED ACTIONS in my equation. Or at least taken a good first shot at it.

"But . . .?" She leaves the space, sensing that I need to unburden my disquiet.

Referring back to the equation, I explain that it still feels incomplete. "There has to be more," I say.

"Surprisingly, the same thing happened with $E=MC^2$. At first, physicists had to recognize the relationship between energy and mass," Carolyn says. Understanding that mass can actually be converted to energy and vice versa was a significant shift in our understanding. Before the late 19th century scientists thought that energy and mass were totally unrelated.

Once it was widely accepted that mass and energy were related, Einstein was the one who tried to understand the relationship of how mass and energy are channeled through the pipe we call the equals sign. That is where the "C" comes in.

I'd known that "C" represented the speed of light, but not why it was important.

Carolyn continues: "By taking the speed of light, just over 670 million MPH, as a multiplier it shows how mass converts to energy."

Noticing that my eyes are spinning around because this is way over my head, she adds: "Think about something you are trying to do, like creating a new product; what allows you to multiply that one action to create an even greater impact? What provides a multiplicative effect?"

As usual, she drops that little ditty of a question on me like a rapper dropping a microphone, bids me farewell and continues on her rounds.

I try to process this as I leave the War Room, refresh my coffee and meander back to my office. Thinking about the multiplicative effect, it comes to me that it is the people I work with.

First, I don't know all of the technical aspects of our products, so I need the R&D folks.

I don't have the time to go sell, so I need the sales team.

I don't know how to run the production equipment. Actually the production staff has banished me from the manufacturing floor because the last time I touched something it caused them two hours of rework. So I definitely need the manufacturing team.

> **Other people are the force multiplier in all we do.**

The thought of the production team automatically makes my stomach twist uncomfortably. Len was a former production supervisor. Worse than a bull in china shop, he was a bull in a glass factory. I was still finding dead bodies around the plant; people that this guy had harpooned.

He would yell at people, tell other departments it was his way or the highway—and good luck if you asked him about the status of an order. People would tiptoe into his office and slink away bloodied. It was like going to see the Soup Nazi, a character from the classic television show *Seinfeld*. The Soup Nazi only waited on people on his terms; if he didn't like how you ordered soup he would ban you from the restaurant and say, "No soup for you."

Len might have thought he was being expedient, but the cost to the business was far too great. Sure he was smart, he knew his stuff and for a while he got product out the door.

But in the long term? We lost good employees who quit out of frustration and we had cost overruns because people wouldn't address problems. Ultimately he became ineffective because no one would work with him. Len was gone before I got to this assignment, but his impact has lasted to this day, and it isn't a good thing.

When I get back to my office I write *RELATIONSHIPS* on the whiteboard. Now it reads:

$$Impactful\ Results = Focused\ Actions * Relationships$$

Clearly we have to be able to leverage our relationships. I stare at the board not yet satisfied.

Carolyn walks in and I say, "Hey, didn't I just see you in here?"

She laughs. "That was the War Room."

I do my best Homer Simpson: "Doh."

She looks at the whiteboard and says, "Hey, your equation is coming along nicely."

I gesture to the chair and she takes a seat. As I explain the latest addition she nods in agreement. Then she says, "It seems like it can be bigger than relationships between people."

At my quizzical look, she explains, "It is interesting when I walk the halls at your company, and honestly at most companies. I hear people talk about how one group doesn't talk to another group. They put up these physical walls, sometimes they are organizational walls or even process walls."

My head is ready to explode when she tells me that it doesn't stop there. One group in the company is known for making people fill out a form before they will even speak to another group.

"There are even groups that talk about each other by what floor they are on—'That's the upstairs group, we are the downstairs group.' You can even see it on the production floor. The preassembly group has a brown floor where the finishing group has a green floor. So they actually call each other the brown floor and green floor groups."

I am about to explode in righteous indignation when I catch myself. I'm guilty of the same thing only with other divisions and the corporate office. I don't talk to the other division heads to share ideas and best practices. Hell, I don't even ask our suppliers for ideas on how we can be more efficient.

The words we use to divide and separate us are ingrained in our language. Words like this group or that group, silos, swim lanes, dominions, turfdoms.

Our conversation continues with a more philosophical bend. We both recognize our need to organize, compartmentalize and create areas of specialty. We need these structures. The problem is when they get in the way, it limits the collective knowledge of the company, it stunts our ability to grow as professionals and causes us to be inefficient.

We start using these structures because of a need for safety. To protect ourselves and wall out others that can disrupt our work. Like how the manufacturing floor locks the doors when they see me coming.

Just like my man cave at home, we all want a place we can call our own that is comfortable and safe from all of our dragons. We spend time decorating it in ways that bring us joy. We secure our territory with walls, doors and buttresses.

Carolyn adds that isolation also erodes trust because over time people talk about "those people over there." We can easily demonize or vilify others as individuals or as whole groups when they are at a distance. If we were with them face-to-face we would see they are people too.

> **!**
>
> **We easily demonize or vilify others as individuals or as whole groups when they are at a distance. If we were with them face-to-face we would see them as real people worthy of the respect we would like.**

It clicks with me because we talk about the corporate finance group as though it is the evil empire. We call them the bean counters as though all they do is count beans. In many cases we don't even know the names of the people we interact with, only their email addresses. I think some of us believe they reside in a secure vault, protecting hordes of cash, and wearing a Darth Vader helmet with a green accounting visor on top. It's humbling to see how I slipped into this type of dogma even though I came from a finance group.

Every year there is this war when we submit budgets. We catapult our budget over the fortressed walls. The corporate finance group in turn retaliates by pouring the budgets (shredded with adjustments) back down on us from the ramparts like hot boiling oil.

I realize that I've never sat down with my counterparts before submitting budgets. No one in my division does. How much time is wasted in the budget war because we can't be bothered to communicate? What opportunities have we missed, and do we really want to wage a war every year?

I realize that the word "relationship" is bigger than just people; it is systems, processes, organizations and even physical space. The force multiplier is *Interrelationships*. If we can leverage our relationships not only with others, but with other systems, companies, and other groups, we can have an even greater impact.

Carolyn smiles and says, "I like it." As she starts to head out the door, she points to the picture of my family on my desk. "Now you need to leverage those relationships to have an even bigger impact."

"You're right," I joke. "I need them to grow up to be successful so they can fund our social security."

In reality, those relationships with my wife and children are force multipliers for me. They give me meaning and purpose. My wife doing what she does allows me to do what I do. I need to make sure I don't overleverage that relationship. If I get that right, my impact will extend well beyond my lifetime.

Time to get home and have dinner with my family, read to the kids and pay back for all I have received. As I leave the office I update my equation to read:

*Impactful Results = Focused Actions * Interrelationships*

I take one last glance feeling satisfied with my work for the day and head home.

As I drive into work in the morning, the sun is starting to peek over the horizon, lighting the sky red and orange. Seeing the sun rise means the days are getting longer, and that I am not waking up too early in a panic of what isn't getting done.

This morning I was able to sit and enjoy my coffee at the kitchen table in the morning tranquility while reading the management book I'd been trying to digest for months. My morning breakfast rested on a plate with utensils instead of on a paper towel with crumbs peppering my lap as I ate and drove to work.

Having had the time to read, breathe and actually digest my breakfast leaves me feeling a bit more centered and less panicky as I drive in today. Instead of fretting over the latest crisis, risks and problems, I'm reflecting on a memorable image from the management book.

In the book, the author describes organizational communication as a spider web. There are strands that emanate from the center but also strands that wrap around in concentric circles. The strength of the web is a function of the strength of the strands but also the structure of the web itself. The more connections, the stronger the web. If you break a strand the web can collapse on itself, undermining its integrity. The spider will work fervently to repair breaks that happen to the web.

I think of the managerial web as larger than just communications. The web can represent the interrelationships in our equation. I realize that in some ways I am the spider of our organization. I am helping to architect our web of interrelationships.

I can see the broken strands. For example, the damage from Len, the former Soup Nazi production supervisor. Len's negative impact lingers even though it's been months since his departure. As a result the sales team isn't connected with the production team.

> **!**
>
> **Organizational communications can have the strength of a spider web when everything is well connected. It can collapse in on itself when strands are broken.**

Further out on the web there are breaks in our relationships with other groups in our company. I wonder why our R&D team doesn't work with the R&D of other divisions to share innovations.

We also need to continue to expand our web of interrelationships beyond the borders of our own company. There are people outside of the company that can have a direct influence on the impact we are trying to create. Why don't we have closer connections with some of our suppliers, or with the university that is only five miles down the road?

At first I have this sinking feeling. How much time is it going to take to fix and build all of these interrelationships? We don't have enough time in the day to foster all of these connections.

Besides, what are we going to do, burn incense and sing kumbaya around the campfire? I am a finance guy; I don't go for all of that touchy feely stuff. And since we are a technology-based company, most of our people are not the warm fuzzy types.

This continues to nag me as I make my rounds during the day. I walk by some of our glass-walled conference rooms and I see teams huddled around the table, engaged in solving some challenge. I see strong threads with lots of connections.

In other places I see people hunkered in bunkers working on something in isolation. Now I am not judging, sometimes we have to lock the door and do some serious thinking. But I am concerned when I walk by Peter's office. He's our head of R&D and one of our smartest scientists.

He always seems to be in isolation, tucked away in a corner of the building. He has good ideas, but I wonder how far those ideas are spread. I don't think he even knows what a sales person is, no less talked to one. Yet his ideas are the future of our product lines. I also know that what he is working on is similar to what one of our other divisions is working on; is it possible that we could get even better product ideas? I see broken strands blowing in the wind around him.

I go back to the War Room and in its emptiness I stare at the organization of the HIPs and actions. How can we build a web of interrelationships that drives this impact? I grab my coffee and go for a walk outside of the building to clear my head. The crisp winter air is refreshing. As I am walking, an idea hits me. I stop at the local craft shop on my way back and gather some supplies.

When I get to the War Room, I pull out a sheet of colored paper and write the impact statement the team created and tape it in the middle of the wall with all of the HIPs and actions. Then I pull out tacks and stick them on each of the four HIP cards. I take four more tacks and stick them on the corners of the sheet of colored paper with the impact statement.

Someone is going to get it for poking holes in the wall.

I reach in my shopping bag and pull out a spool of yarn. I tie an end to the tack on one corner of the impact statement and then unravel the yarn until I have reached the tack on one of the HIP cards. I loop it around the tack, tie it off and cut the strand. I repeat the exercise until I have a strand extending from each corner of the impact statement to each of the four HIP statements.

I then pull out cans of a powdered color spray. I double check to make sure it is not permanent and it is non-staining. As I shake the can, getting ready to paint, Sandra, my admin, walks by and stops in shock, clearly wondering if I have gone off my rocker. Although I explain it doesn't stain and isn't permanent, she still has a look of horror. She closes the door so no one else sees that I have lost it.

I spray a light dusting of concentric color circles, starting at the center and emanating out to the reaches of the four HIP cards. I end up with something that looks like a bullseye painted over all of the materials taped to the

War Room wall. On the whiteboard I have written out our modified equation.

$$Impactful\ Results = Focused\ Actions * Interrelationships$$

I invite the team into the room after lunch to share the work from my arts and crafts time. As they walk in they see the yarn and paint and they too think I have lost it.

I explain the addition of interrelationships to the formula. It is one of those BFOs (blinding flashes of the obvious). We talk about the importance of working with others. Robert comments that too often we let our own agendas get in the way, and when we do that, it ends up costing other people dearly, sometimes costing them their jobs through no fault of their own. I am sure he is also reflecting on his military experience where the consequences were far greater than just losing a job.

Yet we all realize that the broken connections between people persist. Joe pipes in: "We have people who think that they can say anything because they believe they are right."

He shares the story of a previous leader who used the phrase "talk truth to power." This gave some people free rein to say whatever they wanted. People would say, "Hey I was just telling the truth." It was like waving around a machine gun with the safety turned off.

Furthermore, people started to believe they had *the* truth, not a portion of the truth. It also closed people off to exploring others' truths. Joe says that it got to the point where people were mimicking Jack Nicholson's famous quote from the movie *A Few Good Men*: "You can't handle the truth."

The term "power" also implied that some people had power and others didn't. Joe continues: "We need to see that we have power and we need to respect others for the power they have.

"It's not that we need to have everyone doing group hugs every morning. But there needs to be a level of respect in our relationships and conversations that ultimately allows us to accomplish the impactful results we want." Joe gets a gold star for incorporating our impactful results into his reflection.

He decides to coin his own term, and writes on the whiteboard: "Be direct WITH respect."

I explain the choice of the word "interrelationships" extends beyond just people. It encompasses things like systems, processes and organizations. For example, our production process is inefficient because sales has their way of quoting orders. The information then has to be translated so they can run the job. Finance then has to interpret what we shipped and what we are going to bill the customer.

Be Direct WITH Respect.

We had all talked around the excuses. The sales system, the production system and the billing system were all serving different purposes; they were developed by different software companies and implemented at different points in time. I see long broken strands waving in the wind.

The discussion devolves into a debate about finding a new system that does it all. It was the unicorn debate, finding something that solves everything that doesn't exist. Even if we did find it, the implementation would be a cost drain and take forever to implement. Did we really want to divert thousands of dollars from our R&D investments to solve this problem? Plus, corporate was talking about a companywide system for all reporting and management.

We feel hamstrung; the break in this interrelationship between sales, production and finance was holding us back. It also created personnel issues because sales would launch their verbal hand grenades into production for the problems that it created. No wonder they didn't talk to each other.

It's time to take a break so we can refocus. "Let's refresh our coffees and meet back here in 10 minutes," we agree.

When we regroup I turn our focus to the yarn, tacks and spray powder. I explain the image of the spider web and how the yarn represents building our interrelationships.

Karen asks, "So what about the mass of color you have sprayed? By the way, Tom, our facilities coordinator better not see this or he will spontaneously combust."

I explain that the interrelationships of people, systems and processes extend from the center in the following order in the colors I have sprayed on the wall: Intradepartmental is a red band, Interdepartmental is an

orange band, Intercompany is a purple band and Outside
the company is a blue band.

We talk about the importance of the intradepartmental
connections. We have people that aren't connected that
need to be. For example, we have two schedulers that
have their own way of doing things. They can do that
because they work on two different customer sets. Even
though it works for them, it creates issues in production.

As we talk about some of these key connections, I ask the group to write each connection on a 3x5 card and tack it to the wall in the red band for intradepartmental. Joe writes "schedulers" on a card and tacks it up to the wall.

After some discussion we add about a dozen key connections or interrelationships that need to be strong to create our impact.

When we get to the orange band for interdepartmental, all hell breaks loose. The conversation about the conflicts between departments grows and grows. This group doesn't talk to that group. Another group puts up barriers that make it hard to work together. There are always reasons; we all agree it has to stop, but no one knows what to do. I tell them not to worry, let's just tack up these connections that are needed in the orange band for interdepartmental.

A concerning example is the connection between R&D and sales. We never talk about connecting those two groups. They are so different and so separate we are afraid that if we put them in the same room it will create a rift in the space-time continuum.

Robert says: "If we get this one wrong we end up with products that sales can't sell or salespeople selling products we don't make." Diane makes a note to connect the teams together to talk about ideas for future products.

As we move into the purple band for intercompany connections, everyone sees the gaping hole in the connection with the corporate office. There is so much resistance in the room that it could stop a tidal wave in its tracks. There are the usual complaints about all of the requirements corporate puts on us, how they interfere in our business, and how they create more problems than solutions.

Karen jokes about the old saying of the corporate curse. It goes something like this: "We're here from corporate and we're here to help."

Everyone laughs.

I notice that Peter is doodling; he has created a pretty detailed drawing of the Death Star from the *Star Wars* movies with the brand logo for MegaCorp in the center.

I think to myself: Well, there is a message.

I turn the bow of the ship we sail all too frequently, the SS Complaint. I ask: "When do we actually talk to corporate?" The answers are startling, but not surprising. Most exchanges come in the form of emails with a title of ASAP or Immediate Response Required. As we talk about it, we realize that we aren't actually talking to them when we are in email mode.

"Maybe," says Diane, "we should start picking up the phone." Everyone nods in agreement.

"We have become far too dependent on email," Karen says. "Email is a great tool for transactions, for providing information and updates and scheduling times to connect. However, it is not effective in building the deeper interrelationships necessary for our job."

Now she has earned a gold star for incorporating our equation into the discussion. I better stock up on gold stars.

> *"Email is a great tool for transactions, for providing information, sharing updates and scheduling times to connect. However, it is not effective in building the deeper interrelationships necessary for our job."*

Robert adds, "When we do actually talk to corporate, it's when there is a problem or a complaint."

He's right. I reflect on my call yesterday with the finance group. They'd called to tell me the bad news that corporate was putting a 10% task on expenses. That is a nice way of saying, "stop spending." No wonder there are times I don't pick up the phone when I see them calling.

Because our connections are transactions and usually carry a negative load, we agree it is time to start connecting even when there isn't a problem. A great way to start that is with the budget process. We agree to connect with our corporate counterparts prior to the budget cycle to talk about last year, our vision for this year, how we want to work through the process, and find ways to help each other.

Robert adds another example. "There are times when we have an employee complaint that gets elevated to the corporate office. Our contact at corporate only has one side of the story, and we get defensive because they don't see the other side of the issue."

We agree that we can reach out proactively just to let the corporate office know when we see things that might get escalated to them so they are aware. Also, to let them know how we are handling employee issues, and even ask for input so we can manage employee issues more effectively.

During the conversation, a few cards are posted in the purple intercompany band. We also added a few that stretched us beyond the corporate office. For example, one of my colleagues in another division hired a technical person to create integration points between disparate systems so they didn't have so much rework and double-handling of information.

Joe asks if we might be able to have that person on loan for a little while. I say with a smile: "We will never know if we don't connect with them." He chuckles, makes a note and says, "I'll send an email." He catches himself say that as he looks up to see the expression on everyone's face. He quickly crosses off "email" and writes, "phone call."

The blue band for "outside of the company" is a little less obvious. I explain that I picked blue because the ocean is blue and vast. There are lots of creatures in the sea, things we don't normally see. The same is true outside of the company. There are opportunities to create connections or interrelationships, with people and organizations that can help us. Too often we focus on the windshield that is right in front of us instead of lifting our head and scanning the environment around us.

"So," I ask, and gesture toward their impact statement. "Where do you see relationships outside of our company that can help us achieve the impact you have defined?"

A dark hush falls over the room. This isn't something we normally think about.

I continue: "Let's take an example. One of your HIPs is to streamline our production process to make product cheaper, with fewer part numbers and better quality. Fifteen percent of our parts come from ACME Products. They also provide parts and assemblies to a variety of other businesses. They even won an industry quality award just last year. I see their sales person here. I don't think I have ever met their production or R&D people.

Could they provide some insight and even consult on our efforts here?"

That thread causes the darkness to recede and I start seeing the lights go on. The conversations start to build in volume and intensity. Ideas flow. The team builds on the idea of using the technical university down the street. Those engineering students are working with the latest technologies and they have a state-of-the art laser lab that is better than our own.

The team comes up with the idea of forming a student think tank around products, technologies and market needs. They also admit they have never visited the showcase the university hosts every year that demonstrates all the latest innovations they are working on.

That one is a little embarrassing; our founder actually endowed their research lab and we don't take advantage of any part of that.

Diane brings up the other college in our town, a business school and her alma mater. She called herself a library rat when she was working on her thesis. The college has access to databases and resources that would be cost-prohibitive for us to buy. She explains that if we come up with a list of business research questions, the business librarians and students will actually source and compile the information in one package. She also mentions the JJ Hill Library, whose mission is to be a research library for businesses and entrepreneurs at all stages of business.

She mentions that the key to using any of these resources is to have a well-framed and focused set of research questions. "Start with a few select overall questions," she says. "Once you have some information, you can narrow the questions to get more detailed insights."

"For example, if you want to know the size and segments of a particular market, start with that. Once you look at the market segments and select the ones you want to focus on, you can ask specific questions about those segments."

"Start with a few select overall questions. Once you have some information, you can narrow the questions to get more detailed insights."

She uses the example of one of the HIPs: Provide an engaging and impactful experience for all partners. She shares that engagement is a big focus in business right now. One of her professors at the college just published a well-researched whitepaper on the ROI of engagement and the initiatives that can have the best return. "We can start with that article, and also ask the business librarian for help compiling best practices we can use. That way we select a few things that can have the greatest impact and avoid the "flavor of the day" we tend to follow when implementing employee programs. We could probably get a student to work on this as an intern next semester." Another card gets tacked up in the blue band.

The ideas continue to flow. I am amazed at how many resources are out there to help us create our impact. For example, someone mentioned our shipping vendor who makes deliveries every day. They are the logistics experts, yet we don't ask them how we can improve our material handling. We belong to a number of industry groups, from human resources groups to very specialized associations like TAMLM: The Association Of Micro Laser Operators In Manufacturing.

Now there is a conference I need to attend. I am sure they throw some kicking parties.

Kidding aside, all of these associations we belong to are there to serve their constituencies; they have repositories of information available to us and they can connect us with other knowledge experts. Robert mentions that he used to run an industry association years ago and he was amazed at the number of companies that belonged and never took advantage of what was available.

"We don't have time to pursue all of these association resources right now," he points out. "What are two or three that tie directly to our HIPs?" The group identifies two that get tacked up to the blue band.

Our wall is getting colorful. There are color cards, powdered color spray and yarn…it's a bit overwhelming to look at.

It is obvious we are all mentally drained. I suggest we break for the day and regroup in the morning.

I see Carolyn as I head out for the day, the two of us like shift workers passing the time clock as one punches in and the other punches out. "Leaving a little early today are we?" she asks with a smile.

"I will leave you to cover this shift, call me if anything serious happens."

It's nice to leave early for the day, but I am going to miss my late-night conversation with Carolyn. I realize that

Carolyn serves as a connection point in the blue band; an outside resource that can help us with our goals. It is interesting how she has shaped my thinking— and by extension the team's thinking—just through brief, informal conversations. For me Carolyn helps get my brain focused and gives me space to think. She does that in a way that no one else in the company can, because she isn't encumbered by all of the minutia we face every day. One of the interrelationships we could all benefit from is someone outside of our workspace that can create a place to think out loud.

Why would Carolyn want to be that resource for me? Clearly she has an interest in the business she used to work for. Maybe she likes my sparkling conversational skills…OK, that isn't enough. There has to be another reason.

I think back to what Carolyn told me the night I was having an existential crisis. She'd said that she appreciated our conversations, that she asks herself the same questions all the time, and that by talking things over with me she also felt clearer on her own courses of action. We challenge and push each other for the better.

People like to be of service. But discussing business challenges with an outside voice also stretches us in new ways. Besides, who doesn't like to be appreciated for sharing ideas and being respected as a knowledgeable resource?

I remember watching one of those old mafia movies. The boss often had someone they called a *consigliere*, someone who whispered in their ear and advised them. While that might not be the best reference, it suggests that we could all benefit from someone that helps us frame our thinking.

I pull out a note card so I remember to share this with the team. I write: "Find a trusted advisor or confidant outside of work," and "Just ask."

"Find a trusted advisor or confidant outside of work," and

"Just ask."

As I head out into the brisk winter evening the sun is still shining. It is a pleasure to get to enjoy the longer daylight hours. It creates a sense of hope that spring is on the way.

For now, it is time for dinner with my family and some time with the kids. Maybe even one of those workouts on the treadmill that I have heard are so good for you.

After a nice dinner and robust conversation with the family, I take the opportunity to remove the clutter piled on the treadmill and fire it up. As I walk at a healthy pace, I allow my mind to wander back to the progress we are making at work.

The challenge of all the interrelationships continues to weigh on my mind. It seems like there are too many and the framework isn't well constructed. I can see the web collapsing on itself. How do we organize this in a way that we leverage all of the knowledge and resources?

Clearly all of us can make a connection. But the web has to extend beyond each of us. A flash crosses my mind as I realize I have been on the treadmill much longer than I planned. I hop off with more energy than when I started. I make another "note to self" so I can turn my work brain off and turn my "Megan brain" on when I finish my day conversing with my wife.

In the morning it's arts and craft time again. When everyone huddles in the War Room they find I have cut up four strands each of various colored yarns and laid them out on the table. I have put a post-it note with each person's name on our scatter gram of actions. You can see the team wondering what is going to happen today as they glance at the strands.

I explain that we only have so much bandwidth to build these connections. We need to divide and conquer. I assign each person a color of yarn to use and then ask everyone to take one of the four corresponding strands and tie off a connection between their name and the interrelationships that can have the most impact on the results we are trying to achieve.

Joe asks, "Are there any limitations to the connections and how we should assign them?"

I don't want to limit the thinking. I say, "Let's see where you go with this, the only limit is asking yourself which connections will have the greatest impact on the result you have defined." I put emphasis on the words *impact* and *result*.

There are many discussions about who is going to make which connections internally in the organization, with the corporate office and with outside resources. There is even some old-fashioned horse-trading as people vie for connections they want to engage and others that are less appealing.

I am pleased to see the team challenging each other where they see connections that no one wants to create, yet were significantly important to generating impact. For example, Joe talks about a trade organization that has unique resources around process engineering that we can use to improve our manufacturing process. He has already used up his yarn and it seems like a lot of work to establish a new connection that no one knows how to start.

Joe says, "I have heard from an old college friend that this group has two specialists that will come onsite and provide assessments at a very nominal charge. They will do this as part of their connection to a university. They use the assessments for research."

Robert has a strand left and takes it because he knows how associations work and he feels he can frame a charter or engagement description that Joe can approve. Robert also says that by taking the lead with this group it will give him better understanding of and connection to the production group.

I feel like a spider, plucking various strands as we make connections.

As they continue, I feel like a spider, plucking various strands as they make their connections and as they make changes. When they are done, there are some obvious gaps and the team laments at not having more strands. I had a few offers to buy more strands. Of course that came from Diane, our sales leader; always striking a deal.

After much bemoaning Robert jumps in: "We could have more strands if we bring our teams into this process." He asks if we can expand the web if we use our teams.

I agree, as long as we don't overtax the team. "Remember they still have to make the donuts every day." The group agrees, and talks about bringing each team together to do the same thing.

Diane asks: "Is that just for managers, or do we include individual contributors?" There is a healthy debate around this because we can't have every person in the company chasing down connections.

That's when Peter, our introverted, brainiac head of R&D speaks up. Up until now he'd been one of the quieter contributors. I expect him to say that we, as the "smartest ones on the room," can figure this out. Instead he shares a story about an insight that came from an unlikely source.

Late one night, Peter was working in his office on a problem with the new clean room used for highly sensitive equipment. Something was creating unexpected contamination. The facility services person happened by and Peter ended up sharing his frustration with this unexpected guest.

I start to see my friend Carolyn's handprint on the crime scene, but Peter says "he," so it couldn't be her.

Peter continues: "The facilities person explained to me that when he is doing his maintenance work around the building he has to be sensitive to the discharge or blowing from his equipment because it can cause an unexpected mess. He shared, rather humbly, that one night he was using a compressor to clean a vent system and ended up blowing someone's documents all over the office like a Category 2 hurricane. With that he looks up and points out that the heating and air conditioning vent in the ceiling blows right toward the door to the new clean room. He suggested that if they open the doors when the system is running it could be creating the problem."

Peter concludes his story with: "Sure enough, that was the source of the problem and that's how a facilities person who doesn't know our business saved us thousands of dollars."

I think to myself: we aren't paying Carolyn's company enough money.

The team sees that we probably have a broad and huge untapped repository of knowledge and perspective right in the four walls of the company. Peter chimes in again, with another unlikely comment. "I had a professor who once told us that for all of our education and lofty ideas, 'remember that most innovation comes from the front line.'"

Most innovation comes from the front line.

Now that statement is as humbling as it is encouraging. I write a note to make sure that quote makes it to the whiteboard in my office.

"But we have had these meetings before where we bring in our teams to get their ideas without much to show for it," Peter says. "We don't get a lot of engagement or ideas. As a matter of fact, our suggestion box has an accumulated layer of dust that dates back to the early 90s. Although we have paid out some bonuses, we have enough innovation bonus money left over in our budget at the end of the year to fund the company picnic."

Karen seizes on the word "meetings." "Who likes to go to meetings?" she demands. "Plus, our people are so intimidated by the meeting and group setting they don't like to speak up."

Peter adds: "Often the best ideas come from informal conversations between different groups sharing ideas." He continues with another flash of brilliance from a professor who said: "Innovation can come from taking two unrelated things and combining them in a way that creates new ideas." Thus, the facilities person and the clean room.

"Not to mention," Robert says, "money is only one incentive and sometimes the least effective."

Well that put a damper on me—I wonder how much time and money I had wasted.

Diane to the rescue. She shares an approach she heard at conference called "conversation cafes" where people are brought together and they have small group discussions around high-top tables. A topic leader is at each table and people either rotate through the topics or gather around a topic that is interesting to them. You make it informal with food and drink and keep it in small groups. They recommend that people outside of a leadership team lead the discussion at the tabletops.

> *Who likes to go to meetings?*
>
> *Often the best ideas come from informal conversations between different groups sharing ideas.*

> *Innovation can come from taking two unrelated things and combining them in a way that creates new ideas.*

The team loves the idea but everyone is out of yarn. My turn to step in. I tell them that I will work with Sandra to organize conversation cafes after I get their input on topics and discussion leaders.

Since I don't have a piece of yarn, I tell them I will get a lasso to loop around the entire inner band of internal connections for this activity. Diane says she will get me the name of the person at the conference who presented the concept so I can reach out and get ideas on approach.

Before we break, everyone agrees to bring in their teams to review the connections. All team members will be invited to share ideas, but it will be up to the managers to balance who will commit to the connections. However, if there is anyone on the team that has a connection and an interest they will definitely take advantage of that.

Karen volunteers to go get more spools of yarn in new colors for the teams to use. They discuss how many strands each person should get. I explain my logic when I doled out their strands. I'd figured each person could manage three or four connections each, so that is what I used as a basis when cutting the yarn for them. With that in mind, everyone agrees that three or four is too many for the teams because of the limited amount of discretionary time they may have. They decide that one or two should suffice.

As they are talking I am starting to see in my mind's eye how *Actions* ⋆ *Interrelationships* creates a multiplicative effect. Not only have we expanded the bandwidth of the team, but we have a much broader reach to the people, resources and information we need to accomplish the result we are targeting.

I look over at Peter's pad where he has been doodling and drawing as usual. I have to remind myself that this is his way of staying focused and also engaging his creative mind. He has written on his pad "Commit to Connect" in his famous cartoon character font with flourishes and lightning bolts all around it.

I ask him if he would mind sharing what he wrote and why. He explains that all of this discussion reminds him that he needs to remember to commit to connect. Not just with people, but with other processes and other ideas. He says it is easy for him to lock himself in his office and focus on research and forget there are many things that can expand his impact in the company if he steps out of his comfort zone and connects.

! Commitment to Connect

Everyone is energized by this and agree it is a great summary of what we need to do. Peter tears off the page and posts it up on the wall. We agree that is a great thought to end on. We break from our huddle and each person schedules time by the end of the week to build the web with their team.

Over the course of the week I wander by the War Room and see the teams doing their arts and crafts time. I chuckle to myself that it seems we have reverted to primary school by doing this activity. But the energy in the room is very positive. The physical process along with the cognitive process plus the conversations creates a very different level of engagement and focus.

> **!**
>
> **The physical process along with the cognitive process plus the conversations creates a very different level of engagement and focus.**

It even looks different. Usually the War Room is filled with bodies but very little mind, heart or soul. Malaise painted on everyone's faces. People sitting in their assigned seats for another round of death and denial by PowerPoint. And my biggest pet peeve, people working on their laptops and scanning their smart phones.

Don't get me wrong; I don't mind people using the technology. I have actually been pleasantly surprised, usually by the younger generation, who look up the solutions to problems live right while we are in the meeting. However, some don't think people notice when they are scrolling the web, checking email or scanning social media. It is obvious to everyone yet no one says a thing and it is another one of those things that makes my head explode.

The energy in the room shows that by mixing things up and taking a more interactive approach we can amp up the engagement. I am reminded of a colleague who said he changed a lot of his meetings from blocks in hours, to blocks in 5-15 minute intervals. When possible, he would make them stand-up meetings.

The engagement in the conference room this week shows that there is a better way. People are standing up, lively, participating. It actually looks like a meeting I would want to attend, versus the meetings I drag myself to and spend the rest of the meeting looking for the escape hatch.

As I hear these conversations I see virtual strands being strung between people that might not have been connected previously. And the strands on the wall are spreading. Looking from the distance and taking in the whole picture with the cards, the spray paint and the yarn, it seems to form a well-balanced web of connections that surround the impact we are trying to create.

As I gaze through the window of the conference room, my eyes glance past the impromptu sign on the door that says "War Room." It seems as though that term no longer represents what is happening inside those four walls. Plus, "War Room" can be a bit off-putting to some people.

I stand there pondering as Sandra walks by. She admits that she often wonders what goes on in my head. When she asks what I am thinking now, I tell her to "be afraid, be very afraid" in my best Vincent Price evil voice.

I think she is too young to remember that he was one of the first actors cast regularly as a villain because of the deep and malevolent tone to his voice. Clearly that shows my age. She understands once I tell her he was the voice in Michael Jackson's famous "Thriller" video.

As we walk back to the office, I explain what we have been doing as a team and my discomfort with the term

"War Room." She agrees and says she was never fully comfortable with that term anyway. We settle into my office and we continue the conversation about our progress. We are also looking at the whiteboard with our equation:

$$Impactful\ Results = Focused\ Actions * Interrelationships$$

I share with her that I belonged to a group for years that called itself a Think Tank. I used to look forward to sitting in those rooms. I wonder if that might be a good name.

"Why don't you name the room something that uses your term 'impact?'" she suggests. "How about The Impact Think Tank?"

I like it. "Great idea."

She agrees to have a nicely printed sign made to replace the existing sign. Before she does that, she says, "Let me run it by the team first to make sure they like the idea."

Then the conversation takes an uncomfortable turn. She looks at the equation and says it seems as though something is missing. She starts talking about some things that are going on in the culture of the company. There are rumblings of discontent going on under the surface.

Some of it can be attributed to the damage done by the former Soup Nazi Production Supervisor, Len, and some can be attributed to fear for the business. Some of it is the economy, some is concern that corporate is going to shut us down. There are times that rumors run rampant that have little basis in reality. One such rumor is that MegaCorp is going to convert our plant into an operation for the fragrance division and another that says we are being sold.

Where does this stuff come from?

But underneath those rumors are the very real fears of our employees and questions about who we are as a business. As a smaller division, we have always seen ourselves as the redheaded stepchild. Different and separate from the rest.

Which is true, but what they don't see is that MegaCorp likes us for the sizzle of our products and technological leadership.

But if I am honest with myself, some of the concerns floating around are legitimate. The economy is always a wild card; we don't know where things are going to go. Yes, MegaCorp has pondered selling us before, and could put us up for sale anytime.

I thank Sandra for her candor; I always appreciate her willingness to share honestly. She never presents her feedback as a complainer. She is like a triage nurse, keeping her fingers on the pulse of the company and it helps that she has a genuine interest in making the business better. She is only sharing an irregular beat that we need to think about.

We look at the equation and I ask, "So where does all of that fit into our equation?" Both of us realize it doesn't. What is even more disheartening is that we realize that we can have an amazing focus on actions, great interconnectedness and still have the freight train go over the cliff if these rumblings continue. People will lose their engagement, people will leave, and at the first hurdle there will be many people who will give up.

Sandra sees that I have become a bit downcast, and I notice her looking at my scissors. I know she is thinking she needs to remove the sharp objects from the office so I don't gouge my eyes out in frustration.

"Look, the one thing I know about you boss," Sandra says encouragingly, "is that you can figure it out for you. Also, we are big boys and girls; we can figure it out for ourselves too. The first step to a new idea is awareness."

Comforting, but I still think she should remove the sharp objects.

Chapter^5
B = Beliefs

It's been a couple of weeks since I've seen Carolyn. I have been making a more concerted effort to impact myself and my family by seeing the sun shine each day, seeing my family in the evenings and seeing the treadmill.

Tonight I'm back in my office for the late shift. It seems all too familiar—the dark hallways, the empty offices, the sun long since set. I'm hoping Carolyn will be working tonight since I am stuck in my formula and stuck in my head. The noise I hear echoing down the hallway announces her impending arrival. There is no need to put on the pretense of work or busyness any longer. It was OK for her to find me in my thinking pose: feet on the corner of my desk, hands resting on my head, reclined in the high back chair.

She walks in with her usual bounce and air of cheeriness. "That corner of your desk is starting to sink a little lower on that side," she says as she nods at the resting place of my feet.

"I have to favor this side because the other has been sunken down from where I bang my head on the desk," I quip back.

As she chuckles I put my feet back on the floor. "Do you have time to sit and chat?"

She looks over her shoulder dramatically, as though someone is watching over her that might object to her taking a break. "Sure, I don't think I'll get caught."

I toss her a bottle of water from my mini-fridge without asking, and she catches it mid-air. We've gotten good at our routine of pitcher and catcher of water bottles, snappy quips and ideas.

After examining the whiteboard for a moment she says: "You've been making progress. I suppose that is your handiwork I see in the conference room."

I update her on our work around the three parts of the equation. I talk through this as much to solidify what we've accomplished thus far in my mind as I do to bring her up to speed.

> *We focused on solving for impactful results. Check.*
>
> *We created a focus on the key actions using our Highest Impact Pursuits. Check.*
>
> *We flushed out the interrelationships with people and systems that are critical to achieving our goal. Check.*
>
> *We recognized the effect of multiplying interrelationships times our action to expand our bandwidth. Check.*
>
> *We have even engaged the division from the top down, or better yet, bottom up. Check.*

"So what's bothering you?" she asks, noticing the furrow in my brow as I finish my progress report.

"Something is still missing," I say. I recall the conversation with Sandra earlier in the month and relive my frustration all over again. When I take a breath I spot Carolyn glancing around the room the same way Sandra had, wondering if she ought to remove the sharp objects from my reach. But she listens intently, giving me the space to get it all out.

Although everyone is engaged and there is genuine excitement around our progress, I am concerned that at our first obstacle people will the jump the new ship we are building to board the old one, the SS Complaint. I fear things could quickly unravel—everyone in business has seen it happen when you move into the execution stage.

"For example," I go on, "we just received notice of corporate's annual expense task, and this could send everyone in the company a signal that things are not looking good." I don't believe I'm overthinking things; the rumors, conjectures, and exaggerated storytelling are still entrenched in the office culture. Carolyn nods in agreement and confirms my observations. She too has heard these rumblings during her late night rounds.

"Beliefs are a powerful thing," she says. "More than anything else we do, beliefs can blast us through the thickest obstacles or bring even a whole society to a standstill." By way of example, she mentions the consumer confidence index. "The consumer confidence index is only a measure of the beliefs of a whole economy. Yet, it has profound implications to everything around us.

"Remember back in 2008 and 2009 when the market crashed? Think about how we all felt," she says. "People

> *"Beliefs are a powerful thing. More than anything else we do, beliefs can blast us through the thickest obstacles or even bring a whole society to a standstill."*
>
> *Beliefs about safety, security and identity shape how we behave, how we respond, what we say and what we don't say.*

stopped buying and making decisions. Everyone seemed to go into 'bunker mentality;' hunker down and don't stick your head out of the foxhole. The recession fundamentally changed our thinking and continues to shape our thinking today–years later. Even though the stock market rallied and the housing market recovered, many people continue to be shy about buying and investing. It's just like how our parents and grandparents continue to live a life of frugality—even though Great Depression ended in 1939.

"You could be suffering from the same thing we experienced when the markets crashed," she continues. "There are people in this office that lived through the dark ages. I was here when the business collapsed under the previous owners, remember? While it certainly led me to the positive place I am now, I can't pretend that the event didn't stay with me. It was brutal for all involved.

"Even when someone joined the company after the restructuring," she points out, "they would pick up on the cues from the survivors and hear the stories told and retold.

"Some of those stories took on a life of their own—to the point where what's repeated isn't even connected to reality. I heard one person say that when they were handing out the pink slips one of the managers showed up in a grim reaper outfit, scythe and all. I was here and I can tell you, nothing close to that happened.

"And even if they never heard the stories, they have either experienced it themselves or watched family and friends 'made available to their next opportunity in life.'"

"Then we wonder why people are hesitant to commit and why they flinch at the first sign of difficulty. Beliefs about safety, security and identity shape how we behave, how we respond, what we say and what we don't say."

Some stories take on a life of their own—to the point where what's repeated isn't even connected to reality.

While Carolyn's been speaking I've been sinking further and further into my seat. This is way over my head. I am a finance guy. I am not one for chanting around campfires, yet it seems that's where we are headed. I live in a world of debits and credits, profits and losses, balanced balance sheets. This is all too heady for me.

Carolyn sees my eyes spinning and pauses to let my brain digest what my ears just heard.

"I understand," she says, "that this isn't something we talk about in business. Many leaders scoff at this type of talk. Even if they recognize the importance of beliefs, they have no idea how to impact them. Worst of all, they may not realize they contribute to and create beliefs themselves.

"But ignoring it doesn't make it go away. As leaders we need to be hyper-vigilant of our own beliefs and sensitive to what we communicate. Our beliefs scream at people from both our actions and our words. They spill out between the lines of what we are saying. I remember one of the previous senior leaders of the organization came from the sales organization. He carried a personal bias that sales drove the company and everything else was a distant second in importance. His attitude was an open secret; even if he hadn't complained in private conversations that operations impeded sales, it was clearly implied in what he said and how he acted. Everyone knew it.

Our beliefs scream at people from both our actions and our words. They spill out between the lines of what we are saying.

"That created a second-class mentality for everyone else in the organization, and that eroded the foundation of the culture. If you were on the sales team, you could commit murder. Everyone else saw themselves as a day prisoner just waiting for their release at the end of the day only to don their shackles again the next morning. As a result, many people just laid down and gave up.

I nod along to Carolyn's example. Even if it happened before my time at the company, I've seen enough to know that she's right.

"In addition to watching our own beliefs, Carolyn says "we as leaders need to engineer the belief systems and the culture of the business. I remember when the economy took a huge dip and my business was suffering, my mentor would say things like:

> "'Remember it is called a business cycle for a reason. It goes up and down.'

> "Or, 'just remember that most of the money in a business cycle is made at the bottom of the curve, not the top. So when everyone is going into the foxholes to hide, charge forward and take advantage of the opportunities others are missing.'

"My favorite reminder from her was a bit humbling," Carolyn says with a nostalgic smile.

"'Just remember Carolyn, that you are an ant on the picnic table of life; when everyone else is starving, you can survive off of the crumbs left by everyone else.'

"That type of shift in my thinking made a huge impact on my business. I don't want to brag, but when the economy took a dive, I was able to grow my business by 20% that year and profits went up too. That defied logic to me. The difference was what I believed and how it impacted my day-to-day work."

I start to think about the beliefs of my current boss. Somehow Carolyn sees that is where my mind is going. "I hesitate to talk about leaders because that causes people to look up instead of looking in.

We all need to recognize that we lead in some way, from the person on the production line to the executive suite of the company. That means we each have a responsibility to engineer our own belief systems. The first place each person needs to start is not with others, but with themselves."

> **!**
> **Look inward, not upward for leadership.**

She shares a story about the division president when MegaCorp bought the company. "You could tell he didn't like the owners of the company. He didn't say it directly, but he never referred to any of our contacts by name. No, it was always 'they and them,' spoken with the tone of a rebellious teenager. As though MegaCorp was one big unit out to get us. Our enemy.

"People took their cue from him. Everyone started mistrusting the corporate office. And the division president did nothing to quell the discontent between departments. That discontent became all-out war, with mortars being lobbed in daily from all corners of the building."

That hits home. No wonder there was a mushroom cloud hanging over the name "War Room."

"Actually," Carolyn clarifies grimly, "the division president actively encouraged fighting in the name of what he called *coop-itition*, a term he used to describe cooperation and competition. The only problem was the scales were always tipped toward competition with no counterweight of cooperation. As a result no one trusted other departments or even those within their department.

"When the division president was fired and there were signs of a company-wide bloodletting, all hell broke loose. It was like watching the villagers running through town with pitchforks and torches trying to find people to drag to the proverbial guillotine. When the corporate bosses came to visit, you could see the whispering of accusations into the ears of the unsuspecting visitor. You saw people throwing a boss under a bus. Retribution between departments came in the form of ethics complaints being elevated to the corporate office over simple misunderstandings and assumptions that could have been resolved by people talking to each other.

"The culture was toxic, poisoning everyone who breathed the office air. It didn't matter what you tried to do, how you tried to focus the work and even perform the daily work of the company…everything came to a grinding halt. The company culture wasn't spurring people on to do their best. Instead, the culture weighed everyone down and paralyzed them like leg irons. Who could do their best work in that atmosphere?"

I wasn't aware of any of the events Carolyn had just recounted, at least not in any detail. But thinking about it…I did know, didn't I? I had sensed it every day when I walked the halls and felt as though the very air was oppressive and sticking to my skin. I'd heard it in Joe's voice when he accused corporate of stonewalling his efforts. I'd seen how departments went to great lengths to isolate themselves and ice out others.

The bloodletting may have occurred 15 years ago, but in many ways the company had never moved on from that dark period.

I could see my impact on this like the cave hand paintings. Although I hadn't directly told these stories, I had allowed them to happen. I heard them and turned a blind ear toward them.

I also see that I missed my opportunity to create a different impact. Without an alternative, people had no choice but to believe what they heard. I could have, should have but I didn't provide a better narrative. Instead of focusing on the charts and numbers, I would have been better served by engaging with the teams and providing a better alternative to what they thought and believed.

> **Instead of focusing only on the numbers, maybe we need to focus on the stories people tell that limit us and create better stories they can believe in.**

Instead of letting people focus on the negative of the restructuring, I could have shown them where the company was investing in our future. During that time we made a $10 million capital investment in the plant. Instead of focusing on the history of the acquisition and restructuring, I needed to show them how we had a bright future from the capital investments we just made.

Carolyn follows my eye to the whiteboard: "Cash is King. Culture Trumps All."

"See," she says with a smile. "You get it."

Our conversation starts my wheels turning. "What's the difference between beliefs and culture?"

"Great question," she says. "I never thought about it. I am not sure it is a difference between them as much as the relationship between beliefs and culture."

We reflect on the words I had written under the quote: "Culture is nothing more than what we talk about and how we talk about it."

"So if culture is what we talk about and how we talk about it, where do beliefs come into play?"

She lets me simmer and think it through.

An idea, an image starts to bubble up in my mind. I am reminded of an iceberg. It's an effective analogy that people use to describe the small portion we see above the surface and the significant mass below the surface we don't see.

I go to the whiteboard and draw my best rendition of an iceberg, with only the tip visible above the waterline and the large mass below it. It's not very well-drawn but it will do. I draw an arrow to the area above the water and write next to the arrow: "*Culture.*"

Carolyn adds to the idea by saying, "I think culture is nothing but the combined behaviors of the organization. Behavior is what we can see from people, usually in the form of verbal and non-verbal cues that tell us who they are, what they value and what they believe. It is, however, very subtle."

I nod, and inside the iceberg tip I write: "*Behavior.*"

That leaves the rest of the iceberg below the waterline. "I think beliefs are the much larger mass that buoys what we see and experience when working with each other.

"That's where beliefs go." I share my epiphany. "Beliefs are the critical mass that creates the greatest stability of the berg just like they can for the organization."

Carolyn shares a story from an experience she had in the northern Pacific that reinforces our thinking: "I remember seeing a large iceberg floating in a tumultuous storm with 20-foot waves. The boat I was on was tossed about like a bobber. But not the iceberg. The mass below the waterline kept it floating steady."

The visual of the iceberg helps me solidify my understanding of beliefs, culture and behavior.

I go to the whiteboard and write "Beliefs" but am still unsure where it fits in the equation. That can wait for now. I know there is much more to explore. I only have a few synapses in my brain still firing. Time for me to call it a day, and I can see Carolyn needs to get back to her rounds.

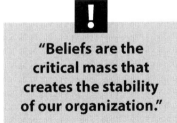

"Beliefs are the critical mass that creates the stability of our organization."

Knowing that there's more to do, I'm reminded that our impromptu sessions always take place on Carolyn's work time. As she starts to head out, I stop and ask her, "Hey, would you be interested in really diving into this topic? I know I could use the help."

Carolyn seems open to the idea, and asks what I have in mind.

"I was hoping we could spend a few hours outside of this office where my mind isn't so cluttered and I am not impacting your rounds. I'll pay you for your time," I add. "Could we find a day to do that?"

"Absolutely," says Carolyn, "but one caveat, you aren't paying me for my time. I benefit from these conversations too, plus it engages my mind in something interesting to me."

I tell her I'll have Sandra call her to set up a time and place. I am reminded of when I told my team to ask for this kind of support and how people are often eager to help out. In any case, I plan to do something nice for Carolyn for taking the time to help me and the company.

Sandra scheduled a very creative venue for my time with Carolyn. She learned that Carolyn is an outdoor type and likes to hike. I think Sandra connected that with the winter weight that had gathered around my belt line. She scheduled us to walk and talk on a hike through a scenic gorge a short drive from the office. Great idea.

We meet at the trailhead on a brisk but sunny late winter morning. The fresh air says that winter is melting away. Because the crocuses are starting to push their way out of the fertile ground, I can tell that spring is right around the corner.

Carolyn sees me looking sheepishly back and forth between my bright shiny sneakers and the trail ahead and says encouragingly, "Not to worry, the trails stay dry year round, plus getting a little muddy can be a good thing. Ready to roll?" That is more of a statement than a question as she starts with a healthy pace.

The walk starts with some idle chatter about the weather, the spring and the history of the glen. Carolyn's familiar with the gorge. She shares the stories that her grandfather used to tell her when they would hike together here. He told her that the local Indian tribes believe that their ancestors pass through these walled cliffs on their way to the great beyond, depositing their wisdom to be discovered by future generations. She wasn't sure if what he told her was the truth (we had just discussed how time and repetition can alter a story's "truth"), but she always liked the visual of passing through the canyons of wisdom and comes here often to see if she can glean some.

Boy do I hope that story is true; but what could these primitive tribes know about solving my problems at MegaCorp?

She continues to explain that the tribes native to this area judged not the health of the people but the health of the whole tribe. Health had a much broader meaning than physical health, integrating what we might call psychological and spiritual health into the picture.

Central to the tribe were their beliefs, which fell in the domain of the shaman. He would listen to the tribal members and maintain the beliefs and rituals to keep the tribe on course. This was important during times of uncertainty.

"Think what it might have been like for them long before buildings and highways," says Carolyn. "There were constant uncertainties. They had to withstand the whims of nature like drought, floods and storms. These events could be disheartening since there was little scientific understanding of how the environment changed, yet their entire existence depended on it."

OK, now I am worried that she's leading me to some spot to perform an ancient ritual dance. I need to tell her I don't dance. I think she senses my discomfort, but persists.

"These tribes didn't have charts and graphs, cash flows and customers. Their needs were much more fundamental. Without the trappings of more modern institutions, they saw what was underneath it all: The importance of their tribal beliefs to the survival of their people. Somehow over the years we have forgotten this."

I reflect on all my education, training and experiences. Nowhere was this ever discussed as part of standard business practices. Sure, the university psychology department dealt with this kind of stuff, but they were intentionally put on the other side of the campus. And let's be honest, we didn't party together.

I know that taking a more holistic view of business health has been growing in popularity in business workshops and books. Heck I owned some of these books. There were the ones with catchy titles that talk about engagement, accountability and purpose.

The problem is, in my experience none of those "touchy feely" insights last longer than the book or workshop. They drain from my brain as soon as I get back to the office and have to answer the call asking for "our numbers." I never had to report any numbers on "beliefs."

Carolyn is still talking as though she's trying to shift my thinking like the switchback trails we traverse up the gorge.

Between her storytelling and my mental gyrations, I don't realize we've climbed quite a distance. The river that carved it out is a couple hundred feet below us. We come to a bend and there is an open area with a view of a waterfall straight ahead. It is breathtaking. We grab a bench so I can catch my breath—and my thoughts, which are whirling around my head.

"I totally get it Carolyn," I begin, not wanting to shut down the conversation but wanting her to understand where I'm coming from. "In concept, that is. But in application I have no idea what to do with this. Sandra's feedback on the currents under the surface in the office has me concerned. I don't see where it fits in the equation and I don't see how it fits into our numbers. Plus, how do we even measure beliefs?"

"Don't get hung up on the measurement part," she says easily, not put off by my pushback. "Remember Einstein came up with his theory long before we could even measure many parts of the underlying equation. Even today, physicists will tell you that for all of our science, we can only explain about 5% of the universe."

!

If we can only explain 5% of the universe, how much of the elements of leadership do we really understand?

That takes me aback. "Really? I would have thought it was much larger than that."

"There is this whole category of dark energy and dark matter, which we know is acting on the universe," she says. "But we can't see it, can't measure it and barely have any understanding of it."

"Are you saying this is all part of the 'dark arts?'" I say with a smile trying to lighten the moment.

She chuckles: "Kinda. Think about all the different measurements we have in business. There are personality assessments, style preferences, employee engagement measurements, and customer experience indices.

"If you ask the statisticians, they will tell you that on a good day, they are predicting only 30% of the variability, and probably much less. What that means is that all these measurements can only give us a glimpse into what creates a given result. Even though we can't measure it today doesn't mean it will always be immeasurable."

"Do beliefs play a role in solving for impactful results?"

"Remember," she continues. "What Einstein was trying to do was explain the relationship between various factors and find a way to solve complex challenges. He came up with a simple equation with deep complexity—and we are still unpacking that equation today. It has shaped the thinking around physics for over 100 years."

Before I can fully process that, she fires a question in a different direction. "Do beliefs play a role in solving for impactful results?"

I respond without hesitation. "Yes."

"Then the challenge is to figure out the relationship between beliefs and the variables you already defined: Impactful Results, Focused Actions and Interrelationships."

Still gasping a bit from the climb, I sit back and ponder the power of beliefs in our business. It is like the waterfall in front of us. Powerful, yet if we reached out to grab it, it would slip through our fingers. Its power has been shaping this gorge for over 300 million years and still shapes it today, relentlessly etching its mark in the bedrock. Although the river below looks calm, it too is shaping the glen, flowing through the rocks and eddies, creating the very beauty we are enjoying.

"The currents of these underlying beliefs are shaping our business just as the water has shaped this gorge," I say, proud of my own insight.

"I'm sure the primitive inhabitants of this area also saw how the beliefs of their people shaped their lives."

"But I am still stuck with what to do with this," I say with more than a little frustration.

"Let's talk about it as we finish our climb to the top. The view from up there is spectacular." Carolyn hops up, ready to charge to the next section. I on the other hand have to push myself off the bench to get in motion.

As we continue our climb, we carry on with the conversation about beliefs. She talks about how the tribes of this area might have discussed challenges such as scarcity of game to hunt or crop failures as well as great joys such as a bountiful harvest or the birth of children. "Now, I wasn't there, mind you." I chuckle at her joke.

She explains that the shaman would have put meaning to the events around them in a way that allowed the tribe to persist in the face of adversity. For example, if a particular type of game was scarce, he might talk about how the spirit world had given the tribe other game to hunt. Or if a crop failed, the trees and bushes of the forest might provide them with sustenance. These tribes successfully survived the ages by using these beliefs long before Europeans arrived.

I reflect on my own religious traditions and how Moses similarly provided strong beliefs that helped the Israelites to escape Egypt even when they wandered lost in the wilderness for 40 years.

Heck. I am just trying to get through the next quarter.

All the talk of "the promised land, the land of milk and honey and the goodness of their God," helped the Israelites survive.

I share my reflection with Carolyn, to which she points out that belief systems can also be equally destructive.

She shares how the beliefs of my company during the dark ages has shaped and may continue to shape our future. "When your division was bought by MegaCorp, many of the people saw the writing on the wall and left for greener pastures. Those that could leave, left. The people who remained lost hope. There was no great leader offering promise for the future.

"I was one of them. There were no jobs for laser physicists at that time, so I stayed and accepted my lot in life until I was washed away in the bloodletting. There are people still at the company that carry that same fatalistic belief and even push it on others. You could see those beliefs eroding the company causing a leak in real talent. Because some people still believe and tell those stories, it can continue to erode the business."

I had seen it happen at companies we studied in university, or companies written up in the trade journal case studies. You could even see it in newspapers when companies started having troubles. A corporation hits bad times, people lose hope and quickly it spirals down. It becomes a self-fulfilling prophecy.

You even see it in sports. You see coaches who inspire hope in their teams. You can also see it in others that are as pessimistic as Eeyore, the negative donkey from the *Winnie the Pooh* books I so often read to my kids. The former will recover from hard times and get better where the latter will continue to turn in lackluster performance.

The sports halls of fame are *not* filled with the names of the teams that have never won a Super Bowl, a World Cup, a pennant or a Stanley Cup. It is amazing to see those belief systems continuously erode teams even when the players, coaches, staff and even owners change.

I have been waiting for the Cleveland Browns to go to a Super Bowl my whole life. Look at the cycle of coaches, players and even owners that have been through that city. They even picked up and moved the whole team to Baltimore and won a Super Bowl within five years. And the expansion team that filled the void in Cleveland hasn't fared any better than before the exodus of the original team. It makes me wonder if it is something in the water in Cleveland. I won't tell Carolyn that one of the eight teams that has yet to win the baseball World Series is also one of my favorites. She might see it is me that is the jinx.

I see the connection and say: "The business leader and the coach are the modern-day shamans, building the belief systems of their organizations."

> *"The business leader and the coach are the modern-day shamans, building the belief systems of their teams."*

I share with Carolyn that I am not one for "the rah rah" stuff. "Too many times it seems disingenuous, fake or Pollyanna. Plus we have real challenges; there is nothing worse than proclaiming all is well when it isn't. People see through that crap and the leader loses creditability."

"What am I supposed to tell the company when we just lost a big piece of business to a competitor? This is very real and we are all scared in cases like this, myself included."

It turns out that Carolyn had a similar experience a few years ago. She had a large corporate client that changed suppliers. (One of those lowest-bidder situations.)

"I had a heart-to-heart talk with my team," she says. "I explained that these things happen. Clients run in cycles. There were things we could have done better, but at the same time we weren't willing to wholesale our business for the lowest possible price and not be able to deliver the service we're committed to providing. If we took the lowest-bidder path it would mean we'd need to start cutting salaries and wouldn't be able to invest in our clients and people."

"So how do you instill hope in that situation?"

"I think that being honest and transparent instills faith in your people," she says. "They see you as someone they might be willing to follow, even if you're lost in the wilderness. We had some tough choices to make.

"I shared my thinking and options with the team. In the end it was a decision we could all live with. It was my decision, but they were a big part of my final choice. The team said they would rather take a cut in pay than reduce the size of the company. Of course, I took the biggest pay cut.

> *Being honest and transparent instills faith. You will be seen as someone they might be willing to follow, even if you're lost in the wilderness.*

"I also borrowed against the line of credit, not something I like to do. But what was really heartwarming was how the team freed me up to go find new business. I even had one employee provide an introduction to someone they knew that handled facilities for a large company. We ultimately got that business and that employee got a nice bonus. We recovered but it took some time. Eventually I was able to restore the pay cuts and repay the lost wages to them."

We have reached the top of the trail and the source feeding the cascading falls and winding river below.

Standing atop a large plateau, we can see the gorge unfold below us. It is a spectacular view that goes on for miles. Because the trees have yet to bud, we can see the full contour of the gorge. You can see how the water has carved and shaped the landscape over miles and for millions of years.

The effect on my brain is equally expanding. I can see the long view, not just of the landscape, but the long view for the business.

"Spectacular isn't it?" Carolyn says.

I nod, and we both stand in silence, taking it all in.

After a few minutes, Carolyn strolls to a picnic bench and unburdens a backpack she was carrying. She pulls out some food and drink and spreads it on the table. Thank goodness she thought of this; I am famished. I was too self-absorbed in my own thoughts to even notice she was carrying a backpack.

We shift to more personal territory. I ask her about her husband and children. She seems to also enjoy a good family and a supportive spouse like me. She has three children, a daughter in that teen transition and two boys, a four year old and a seven year old. I comment that I had seen a laminated photo of the kids and her husband on her equipment when she rolls through the office.

"I take them with me to every job site to remind me why I am doing what I am doing," she says.

"Is that something everyone does at your company?" I ask, having seen similar laminated photos on other employee's equipment.

"We don't make it a requirement, but I have the portable laminate family photos made for anyone who wants them."

I ask her where she met her husband and surprisingly, they met at the division I was running. They started dating after he left for greener pastures. He now works at the local university teaching chemistry. She talks about how she and her husband love to hike, which explains why she is kicking my butt on this climb. The kids love to go to the zoo throughout the year, even in the winter months, and the whole family considers themselves to be amusement park junkies.

Carolyn's flexible schedule allows her to attend her children's events. I ask her how she manages to keep the stress down with all the demands of her business and her family.

"Stress is a state of mind, a belief if you will." I look at her a bit skeptically as she continues. "Have you ever seen someone encounter great difficulty and take it in stride, while someone else experiences a less dramatic event and freaks out? I think that the beliefs underneath drive how the person responds.

"Heck, we see it in business too. Challenges arise every day; some organizations take it in stride, while others turn it into a major drama worthy of a Hollywood screenplay.

"I think one of our core beliefs is related to how we perceive our control on the world around us. When I was stressed about my school deadlines, my mother used to say, 'Remember, stress isn't about workload; stress is about control.' So I try to keep a clear eye on what I can control and try not to bark at the moon about those things that are out of my control."

Now that is a powerful belief. I am reminded of how much time we spend complaining about all the things that are outside of our control. "But there is so much we can't control that impacts our quality of life."

> **Stress isn't about workload, it's about control.**
>
> **Stress is a state of mind . . . a belief.**

"Of course," she says. "But we always have control somewhere."

I toss back one her stories as a challenge. "What about your infamous vacation fiasco?" During one of our late night chats, she had shared a recent vacation her family had taken when flights were cancelled and they were stuck in the airport overnight.

"Did I have any control?" she asks.

"Of course not," I answer, "you were a victim of the weather."

She laughs lightly. "Victim is a choice you have control over."

"Ok wise guy, where did you have control in that mess?"

"Well the first was figuring out our options, like alternative flights, renting a car or finding a hotel."

With my best gotcha voice I say, "But you were screwed, you said you spent the night in the airport."

"Well once we exhausted those possibilities, we had control over what we did with the time. We made it an adventure with the kids; we told stories and played games. One game we played involved making up stories about the people around us. I learned how creative my kids really are. We even talked with an interesting couple with two kids the same age as ours. They were from another country and we would never have met them had we not been stuck. My kids learned how children from other countries like to play. All of this showed how we could take advantage of something right in front of us instead of being blocked by all the shadows of misfortune."

Wow, that's humbling, I think to myself. How often do we miss what is right in front of us, for all of the complaining and whining about those things that we can't control? I almost see all of our corporate expenses pouring past us in the cost of lost opportunity.

"At one point we were sitting next to this bickering couple who were complaining about everything," Carolyn continues. "So we got up and moved. See, one of our choices is the choice of what we believe and what we take in from others' beliefs.

"You may not be responsible for what happens but you are responsible for what you believe and how you choose to respond. I am hoping that my husband and I showed our kids that they can choose how to respond in adversity."

I think about how Carolyn and her husband modeled for their kids how to manage the unknown and unexpected. It makes me realize that others are probably watching me when something happens to see how I am going to respond. My response probably cascades through the organization like these falls through the gorge.

She continues: "My grandfather told me when I was young that being a victim is a choice of what you believe.

And that came from a man who lost his right arm in the war, long before we had the technologies we have today for prosthetics. It was also long before companies were more accommodating to people with disabilities. He relearned how to play the piano, he played golf very well and he had a successful career as a delivery person for a package company. Oh yeah, and he was Mexican-American, so there were many cases when he had to work against what others might automatically believe about him as well."

Victim is a belief, a choice, that you have control over.

Ouch, she got me on that story.

I start to realize how much time the leadership team's spent—even worse, how much time I've spent—believing we were victims of everything from the corporate office, to the whims of our clients and the economy. "So if, for example, 'victim,' is something we choose to believe, what is an alternate choice?"

"That is the role of the shaman, to replace the limiting beliefs with better beliefs. Beliefs that support the impact you are trying to create, not undermine the very ground you are standing on."

With that she pops up from her seat and starts to repack her backpack. "Time to descend back down the trail."

I had forgotten that we were only half done with our hike. After the first half, I'm not popping up from anything.

We stop one last time to take in the amazing view of what has been carved from the landscape. I tell myself that I believe I can make it back down the gorge without passing out from exhaustion.

Although I am not sure I fully believe it yet.

Our descent down the gorge is mostly spent in light discussion, stopping occasionally to admire the topography and scenery. Seeing the shaping power of the water is a strong metaphor for our company's beliefs. It is clear to me now that more than anything, our beliefs shape the path of our business.

Unexpectedly, the hike down through the gorge is even more difficult than the climb. The constant pounding of our feet on the trail is necessary to keep us from falling headfirst. It requires a whole new set of muscles and I can feel the fatigue in my legs.

Carolyn shares a cautionary tale her grandfather told her on one of their hikes. Local tribes used to run races up and down the gorge as a test of stamina and strength. A young boy once fell into the gorge while racing down. The legend says that his voice can be heard echoing in the rapids below, reminding people to be equally cautious running down as they are when they are racing to the top. "I think he was trying to keep me from being reckless on our hikes."

That little ditty has me more than a little worried.

"I didn't mean to scare you, I only wanted to remind us that we need to keep our focus and be cautious. This isn't as easy as it looks." As if to tug me away from my apprehension, she shifts gears a little. "It is also a good reminder that when we dig deeper into people's beliefs, we should be equally cautious. It can be more difficult to truly understand what is underneath the surface of beliefs than it is to lift up new ones."

> *We need to be cautious as we dig deeper into people's beliefs.*

As we pass by the falls we'd stopped at on the way up, the breeze through the gorge shifts and carries the mist directly into our path. The mist clings to us and permeates every part of us. At once it is refreshing and cleansing. But also a bit annoying as it fogs my glasses.

"If our beliefs are the water in the river and the falls, this mist must also be part of our beliefs," I say.

"It is interesting how beliefs create cultures that hang in the air like this mist," Carolyn says. "Clinging to everything. I can tell you that when I go into a client I can feel the culture in the air. It may sound strange but it really does permeate everything and you can feel it."

She's right; I remember the feeling the first time I came into this division. I couldn't put a finger on it, but I could feel the culture washing over me.

At last we reach the parking lot and we take a bench at the trailhead. The babbling brook flows gently past us, not revealing its shaping force that only moments ago was carving the gorge we climbed.

"So I can see how our beliefs shape our company," I say, "but I still don't know what to do with these beliefs."

"Before you worry about that, think about where you'll put beliefs in your equation? Maybe that is the best place to start."

"Good question, what do you think?" I ask. The question hangs in the air between us. Either she knows and isn't answering or she doesn't know. Maybe she's giving me time to reflect.

"We decided that interrelationships can have a multiplying effect on our focuses' actions," I say out loud. "Which is why we decided on Actions * Interrelationships. Beliefs now seem to have an even more powerful effect on the results. I would dare to say an exponential effect. It seems that if we don't have a strong belief system it doesn't matter what actions we take. So maybe beliefs are an exponential effect on actions."

Then I stop to think about our relationships. There are people that seem to be surrounded by a mist of negativity—and who spread it wherever they go. You can see it soaking into other people. Then each person in turn spreads this mist cloud to others.

I think about a supplier who comes into our plant to service our equipment. He's always complaining about something. Not just the equipment, but anything from the weather to politics. You can watch the productivity drop after he leaves, as though his cloud of negativity weighed everyone down. So clearly beliefs can have a profound impact on both the actions we try to take as well as the relationships between people. Our beliefs also impact our ability to seek out and work with other organizations. If we see the corporate office as the evil empire, none of us will pick up the phone to talk to them.

I share my thoughts out loud with Carolyn and conclude that our Actions * Interrelationships should both be raised to the power of our beliefs.

"I am starting to see how our beliefs can have a profound impact on our business," I say. "If we can do something with this, we can carve a deep impact on the business. I need one of those people you talked about that each tribe had, what did you call him?"

"A shaman," she says. "But you don't need a shaman, you need to see yourself as the shaman for your business. Any one of us can find ways to build beliefs that help us, and get rid of the ones that hold us back."

"So how do I do that?" She can see the doubt in my eyes. It's like she can tell that I am thinking I need to come up with some primitive ritual, dance around a campfire and tell prophetic tales.

"Don't worry, you aren't going to have to become a mystic of sorts. I think what this means is that you become much more aware of your beliefs and the beliefs of your people. Once you can see them, you can start finding ways to build better beliefs for the company. That might be a conversation for another day if you want."

"OK, I'll buy into that."

We finish our walk with some light discussion and start to prepare to leave the tranquility of the park. I thank her for her time, her insight and giving me a place to figure this out. I commit to have Sandra schedule another get-together.

As I drive into the office I am very mindful of the contour of the landscape. The creek that flows from the gorge merges with another creek to form the river that winds into our city. You can see where communities and industries popped up along the water and how it has fed this community in many ways.

I realize that our beliefs flow through our company just as this river flows through this town. A rather ominous thought creeps in to my mind. Back in the 1960s this river had become so polluted from industry that it was declared dead, nothing could live in it. Only a couple of decades later, the beliefs of this company too had become so toxic the company was near death. It took time to dredge the river bottom, stem the flow of toxins and create better ecological practices. Only then was the river brought back to life. It serves as a good reminder for me and my business challenges: never let the pollution get that bad. And it makes me realize that I need to be patient because it will take time to build a strong belief system as a company.

When I get to my office I look out the window and realize that I have had a beautiful view of this river all this time and never taken notice. Never seeing how it has shaped everything around me. As a matter of fact, this company was founded on this spot over 50 years ago because it needed access to the waters that flowed through here.

Sandra walks in and takes notice of my casual attire and the mud splattered on my pant legs and sneakers. "How was your hike?" she smiles, probably thinking she had the fun of inflicting this jaunt on me.

"Actually very refreshing. Worthy of a couple of hours this morning."

After we catch up on the morning's events and calls, she departs, closing the door behind her, and leaving me with my thoughts.

I go to the whiteboard and complete the equation demonstrating the power of beliefs.

$$Impactful\ Results = (Focused\ Actions * Interrelationships)^{Beliefs}$$

I settle back into my chair in my thinking pose and start pondering how to leverage these beliefs so we can release their exponential power. This is going to take some serious thinking.

Clearly beliefs can have an exponential impact on what we do (actions) and our connectedness (interrelationships). Conversely, a negative set of beliefs will undermine any action we take and any connections we try to build.

Beliefs can have an exponential impact on what we do and our connectedness. Negative beliefs can undermine any action we take and any connections we try to build.

Having spent enough time in the theoretical though, it is time to grab my armor and head out to slay some dragons. My casual appearance will be a surprise to those who never see me without a pressed shirt and tie. Oh well, I am sure they can handle it.

Chapter 6
Formulating Beliefs

As I walk the hallways I can hear the beliefs of the people pounding away at the foundations of the company like the falls carving the gorge.

I sit in on the R&D meeting and listen to a conversation:

"But we don't have the money that our competitors have to develop this type of product," I hear from one of the research engineers. The feeling of refreshment I had when I entered the building chills. As I'd told Carolyn: the warm fuzzy stuff is hard to hold on to once you're back in the real world.

But then Peter, my introverted head of R&D pipes in. "But we don't have the overhead and bureaucracy that our competitors have either," he points out. "I was at a conference once and a peer from one of our competitors was talking about the layers of approval that are needed just to consider a new idea."

Bam! Peter, with two sentences, is starting to erode a boulder of opposition.

One of the engineers sees me in the back of the room and says to me: "So you can approve whatever we want?"

Uh oh, warning, this is a set-up.

Peter jumps to my rescue: "It isn't what you can get approved, it's what you can justify. We don't need to ask for a blank check. Remember the sophisticated technology we use was invented in someone's garage. The solution doesn't exist in a checking account, it exists in our brains."

I think I just saw a boulder split from the power of one person's beliefs. After a little more discussion, I decide I should get out of the way. They have this.

> *Bam . . .*
> *one sentence can break a boulder of opposition.*
>
> *"The solution doesn't exist in a checking account, it exists in our brains."*

I hear more beliefs cascade through the organization in the form of casual conversation as I walk through the hallways wearing my invisibility cloak (or close enough—between the casual clothes, the mud-splattered pants and the slightly still-misty glasses, only the people I work closely with would recognize me).

Some beliefs are quite scary. I overhear one person say to a colleague: "The person in IT is just trying to set me up to fail." And the person sitting with them doesn't even challenge the statement.

A little while later I overhear someone in a team meeting crack: "Look guys, we need to get this cost reduced so the company can buy another jet for the executives."

I even hear someone say casually over lunch: "I don't think the company would care if this whole department is cut."

Of course no one says these types of things when I am around in pressed shirt and suit mode. Everyone smiles and says how great everything is and how much they are committed to the company. I am reminded of a guy I worked with early in my career who would be the first person to speak up at company meetings with something positive. However, in the dark hallways of the office he would say things like: "There are only two kinds of people who care about the company: owners and idiots."

As I retreat to my office with a gloom hanging over my head, Sandra follows me, sensing I need to get something off my chest. When she asks me what's wrong, I unload the stream of things I had heard in the hallways. That, combined with our discussion the other day has me a bit disillusioned. It seemed the progress I'd made during my hike with Carolyn has been washed away already.

Sandra shares her squeaky wheel analogy—but with a little bit of a twist. "Look, what you're hearing is the equivalent of the squeaky wheel. Remember you aren't hearing the parts that work smoothly. Of course there are negative beliefs under the surface, but it isn't everywhere."

I add that no one is even challenging the negative statements. They just accept them as truth and fact.

"I know," she says, "but remember that when information is missing people fill in the gaps, and usually it is with assumptions of the worst-case scenario."

She shares how she was waiting to hear about a job once, and the interviewer didn't call when they said they would. Sandra started making up stories to herself about what went bad in the interview and how the interviewers didn't value her as a candidate. She went even

!

When information is missing people will fill in the blanks and too often with negative assumptions.

139

further, convincing herself that she didn't want to work for a company that couldn't keep commitments. She finally got a call; it turned out the reason for the delay was due to a major systems outage that had the whole company scrambling. She admits she felt a bit foolish.

"But how many times do we lack information and start making up stories?" she says. "We do it easily—and it doesn't take long for those stories to become true in our minds."

I realize that if left unchecked, stories can have a powerful erosive effect. As if sensing my thoughts, Sandra adds:

"Remember, that there are also positive things that flow through the organization. For example, when you promoted Peter to the head of R&D, people in the company got excited because they know he is brilliant. It created hope for the future of the business. Don't think it is all bad. The good things have an equally positive impact."

She makes a good case. I have work to do and calls to return, but when Sandra leaves I feel a little lighter.

Later in the day we have a staff meeting and I watch the stream of beliefs cascade through. It is amazing how subtle it is. Like the waterfall, you can't reach out and grab any part of what is pouring through the conversation. However, they have just as much power as the falls and river that formed the glen.

We are in a heated discussion about the corporate task to take out 10% of our cost by year-end. I watch the conversation and admit that too often I have allowed it to flow its own course. On more than one occasion I've let myself get caught in the currents of these conversations that end up carrying us away into Class IV rapids.

After a while I stop the discussion and suggest we take a different angle. "What are we telling ourselves here?" The group looks at me a bit stunned, again wondering if Sandra has spiked my coffee.

"Just throw out what comes to mind. Let's free flow, no judgment, not good or bad, let's explore what is the current underneath the conversation we are having?"

> *What are we*
> *telling ourselves?*

I give them an example of something I am telling myself. "I was walking around today, and in hearing some of the side conversations, I feel like no one in the company cares about what we are trying to accomplish. As a result, people will only protect their fiefdoms when we try to make cost cuts."

Once it gets started, it is amazing how easily it pours out. I can tell that we all feel a bit humbled; because when we say these things out loud we have to own them. Because the cost reduction was such a significant issue that concerned everyone, of course the list was fairly negative. When we were done we had filled up a couple of flip charts of belief statements. For example:

Departments will not work together to find cost savings.

Corporate is just in it for the money.

They don't care about us.

They don't understand our business.

The market is challenging right now, and they are making it harder.

Our competitors are going to eat our lunch.

We have always been the redheaded stepchild.

Our market is dying.

We can't cut our way to growth.

Interestingly Diane, our head of sales, chimes in with a rather shocking and vulnerable statement.

I am not sure I can meet our numbers as it is, and I am even more concerned if I have to cut expenses.

The rest of the group chimes in to reassure her. Not reassure her that she can get it done, but that they too have their own fears. It starts with a discussion about lack of confidence in their team, but more than one person, myself included, admits our own uncertainty.

I look at the list, consider the conversation and think that I now need to have the sharp objects removed from the conference room too. I am uncomfortable because this isn't the typical conversation about tactics and strategies. It seems like a bit of group therapy, but I will admit it is cathartic.

We are motivated by fear and that can be scary, but also it can propel us. As we learned in high school biology, fear is hardwired into our DNA. When we are in fear mode we can decide to fight, flee or even freeze. Talking about all of this seems to be creating a swell of fear. But surprisingly, that swell seems to push us toward fighting, not with each other but fighting for the impact we all want to have. It brings the group together.

I am reminded of a scene from the movie *Apollo 13*. A catastrophic failure nearly ended the lives of three brave astronauts. When it was clear they were in danger, bickering ensued. Jim Lovell (played by Tom Hanks) stopped and asked the other two astronauts, "Gentlemen, what are your intentions?" They stopped in their tracks, wondering what he was asking. Without waiting for their answer, Lovell said, "I'd like to go home." In that moment Lovell pivoted them from fear to purpose.

> **Fear is a powerful motivator, but we can use those beliefs to propel us.**

Even though this team isn't bickering, there is a fog of fear hanging in the room. I sit forward to the table and rest my elbows. Not trying to mimic Tom Hanks or Jim Lovell, I decide to lean into the fear.

> *"Gentlemen, what are your intentions?"*

"I get it, we are all afraid, and there is much to be afraid of. The question we need to ask ourselves is, do we want to flee or fight? Any one of us could leave here tomorrow and land another well-paying job. Believe me, I have considered it."

Everyone looks shocked by my revelation. First that I would consider leaving, but more importantly, that I would say that out loud. I think it is a good shock because it shows we can all be human and have our doubts and fears.

> **We make choices, every day, every hour, every moment about what we choose to believe. What are you choosing? Is there a better choice?**

"But I have to make a conscious choice at those moments: Do I want to give up the fight? Do I think we can do this? What impact do I want to make and leave at this company long after I am gone? Allowing those doubts and fears to permeate our brains can erode our focus and undermine our efforts. What is even more concerning is that our teams can sense it just like a deer in the forest senses danger. They may see it in our eyes, in our body language or between the lines of what we are saying.

"If we have these doubts, I guarantee our people are having the same thoughts." Ouch, did I really just say all that? It is time to pivot and dig out of the hole I just created for myself and the team.

"But any belief can have a counter belief. We can choose different thoughts. It is a choice we make every day, every hour, every moment. Ultimately it is a choice of what we do with these things we tell ourselves. It reminds me of the quote in my boss's office that was attributed to Bob Proctor. In bold letters it said: 'Faith and fear both demand you believe in something you cannot see. You choose.'

"We need to ask ourselves, I would even say *challenge* ourselves, to look below the surface and decide if we believe that we can do this, if we believe our teams can do this and if we believe that there is a market opportunity for us outside these walls. If the answer is no, either we pull up the tent poles and pack it in, or we need to change our beliefs. Not to be a fountain of quotes, but I always liked Henry Ford's quote, 'Whether you think you can, or think you can't—you're right.'

"I'm not asking you to answer now, but I want you to write down those three questions." I repeat them again to give them time to capture then.

Do I believe I can do this?

Do I believe the team can do this?

Do I believe there are opportunities for our company to be successful?

"I am also not asking you to be Mary Sunshine either. We need to recognize that there are times when we will be unsure. Don't let it lurk in the shadows. Let's get it out into the light and see if those beliefs stand up to our scrutiny."

I continue: "The most important question we can ask ourselves when we dive into these beliefs is, 'Is that true?' I have to admit, sometimes I'll tell myself something, but once I really think about it, I can see that it isn't true.

*Do I believe
I can do this?*

*Do I believe
the team can do this?*

*Do I believe
there are
opportunities for our
company to
be successful?*

"Knowing that we all have doubts and fears and the rest of those beliefs," I say as I wave my hand toward the flip charts, "we can make a choice, a choice of what we want to believe."

I let the team ponder and absorb not only what I said, but what's written on the flip charts. Now that the beliefs are all on the flip charts, they could no longer hide in the dark recesses of our minds. These beliefs have to stand in the scrutiny of the daylight. As I look at the list, it is clearer to see how these ideas and thoughts pound away at us all day, eroding our energy and confidence. If these beliefs have the power to carve out our culture, can we also create beliefs that carve a different path, an even better path?

After a break to refresh our coffees and brains, Robert steps forward and grabs the marker. "Let's look at these and talk about what could be a better alternative than what we are telling ourselves, and see what might help us drive the organization to better results."

One by one the team starts formulating substitutions to some of the more limiting beliefs. One of the toughest ones is the feeling that we don't belong, "the redheaded stepchild" syndrome we have been suffering from.

Diane responds with several alternatives, such as "we are unique and special in what we do; we are small and we are nimble."

I remind myself that I need to apologize to all the redheaded stepchildren out there.

Karen tackles the heartless, money grubbing, Death Star of a parent company to which we are beholden. I have to admit that this is a hard one for most of us.

She reminds us that MegaCorp is a publicly traded holding company. Because her husband is the CFO for a major company she has learned that every day the corporate executives get pounded on to meet financial projections. Financial analysts are poking at their business model to make sure it is sound. Institutional investors, who have a responsibility to all of their investors, need to ensure they meet their earnings projections. That is why we are repeatedly asked about projections. "My husband said the other day that before they walk into an earnings call they prepare answers for 150-200 questions they may get. They have to be prepared for anything.

"Of course the markets want to see growth and profit," Karen explains, "but you know the biggest challenge they face? Consistency. The markets hate it when you miss your numbers. As you would expect they hate when you come in under your projections, but they also get concerned when you always exceed them or if you exceed them by a large margin because it shows you aren't on top of things. So that is why we get the constant calls about 'the numbers.'"

The group sits back and takes in this other perspective. The room seems to lighten a bit.

Peter jumps in and says, "It is disheartening though, when we are making our numbers and we still have to reduce costs by 10%. That makes my people wonder why we have to suffer because other divisions are missing theirs. That contributes to the redheaded-stepchild syndrome."

Robert jumps in again because he has the marker and holds the position at the front of the room. "I can relate Peter, I get the same pushback from my team. Sometimes I have to remind them, and myself quite honestly, that there were times when we were losing money and had to rebuild this division. Other divisions had to take cost cuts to keep us afloat. That is why the 'I' in interrelationships is so important. We don't live in a vacuum."

OK, time for me to break out the gold stars again.

I recognize Robert for reminding us of the relationship between the different parts of the equation. Beliefs impact interrelationships and actions. This is just like interrelationships impacting actions. It is all connected.

Peter nods slightly as he, and the rest of team, get a better understanding. So Robert continues. "Given everything we discussed, what can we be telling ourselves and others that is a better alternative to our belief that our corporate parent is made up of money grubbers?"

What can we be telling ourselves that is a better alternative?

After some discussion the team comes up with a pretty robust statement: "By being consistent in our regular projections, it allows us to work with corporate to meet their investment goals and opens the door for corporate to help us with our investment needs."

We take some time to continue to tackle some of the other more challenging beliefs before we break for the day. The team agrees that this was helpful for them, but also that it would be a worthy exercise for their teams.

Diane reflects on an experience with her team. "This requires me to be vigilant. I can see how these thoughts can sweep through our subconscious like the Ebola virus."

"This requires me to be vigilant. I can see how these thoughts can sweep through our subconscious like the Ebola virus."

She shares an experience from the sales meeting last week. One of the sales people was very vocal in raising concerns that they couldn't displace a competitor at one of our clients because we didn't have the features the other product had.

"That started a groundswell from the rest of the team. The meeting devolved into self-flagellation that made me wonder if any of the sales people would even pick up the phone to call a customer that day. Fortunately we had Peter attending our meeting for the first time. He told the team that because we are a smaller company, we can make modifications to our design quickly; so if they felt they wanted a feature, his R&D team was ready to come up with some specifications. Was I glad we connected sales and R&D. That interrelationship is critical to us."

Now Diane gets a gold star for taking the initiative of building the interrelationship between sales and R&D.

"Sally, one of our newer reps chimed in too. She said that her experience shows that we can't sell what we don't have, so we need to focus on what we do have and sell that. As a new person, she felt confident in the capabilities and features we have. Although she had run into this other competitor, she saw where they're missing capabilities our products have.

"I have to admit I felt saved by Peter and Sally," Diane concludes. "I have seen other meetings degrade quickly when subjects like this are raised and as a result, sales efforts slow down."

This has proved to be a healthy discussion. I wrap up by saying; "I think we have all had meetings disintegrate under the weight of these types of discussions and the underlying beliefs. It can be very subtle and spin out of control quickly. I have seen people state a belief as a fact and before too long it is written into the corporate lore in permanent ink. I agree with Diane, this requires our constant vigilance. Let's agree that although we worked through a number of beliefs, this isn't a once-and-done effort."

> **!**
>
> **Sometimes beliefs get stated as facts and end up written into the company persona in permanent ink.**

Although it might seem like a negative, we agree to leave the flip charts in the room and keep them in the light of reality.

Diane says, with some concern, "But what if our team sees these, what will they think? Aren't we just propagating negative beliefs?"

It's a great question and a valid concern.

"Well," I think out loud, "my guess is they are already aware of these thoughts from us, so it might not be a surprise. It's also likely that they have similar thoughts. Maybe because we are adding in alternatives, it will help the team build a stronger culture of beliefs. Most importantly, we need to be real. If we're real, it helps others be real. We don't have to hide behind our superman uniforms. We are human like everyone else. Heck, I would even invite them to add to the list and help come up with better alternatives."

"What are we telling ourselves?"

"Is it true?"

"Is there a better alternative?"

That is a good note to finish on and we break for the day. By way of summary, I suggest that there are three questions we can ask ourselves and others when we run into a belief.

"What are we telling ourselves?"

"Is it true?"

"Is there a better alternative?"

Peter scribes them on a flip chart, and posts it on the wall.

The day has wound down and I am yet again alone with my thoughts. I am in the room formerly known as the War Room, now called the Impact Think Tank or ITT for short. I am looking at the beliefs on the wall, trying to distill this down to something meaningful. Like clockwork, Carolyn comes strolling through the office and catches me with my feet up on the table. She's waving her air quality wand through the air again.

"Is it getting any better?" I ask, my question more as a metaphor about the quality of the cultural air around the office.

"Much," she says.

"What is this new stuff?" she asks as she gestures toward the flip charts with the belief statements. Inadvertently, she waves the hand holding the wand. The effect is rather dramatic.

"Can you suck some of the toxins out of that stuff?" I ask.

She smiles and nods with an invitation for me to continue to explain. I toss her a cold water from the fridge as an invitation to grab a seat.

After I summarize what the team and I have been working on around our beliefs, she sits quietly and absorbs the broad spectrum of beliefs we have identified.

I continue to explain that it feels like there is more under the surface here. She agrees: "I think there is always more under the surface. Our beliefs are very complex and built up over years from all of our experiences, just like the river that carved the gorge we hiked."

> **!**
> **The beliefs can be like a puzzle where you have to find the pattern.**

"It seems that there is a path or direction to these beliefs," I say, and add, "But it is like one of those puzzles where you have to find the pattern but you can't see it. I can't quite put my finger on it. At times I feel like the team loses hope. I know I need to inspire hope but it is like the mist in the falls, I just can't grasp it."

"Hope can be complex, but by definition it is fairly easy," she says. "I had a friend who used to say that 'hope lies at the intersection of enduring and encompassing.'"

Hope lies at the intersection of enduring and encompassing.

I have to record that, even though I am not sure what it means. I go to the flip chart, write it down and post it on the wall. "Can you explain that more?"

"When people are hopeful they see good things in two ways. First they see good things as encompassing—as in, they permeate all parts of their life. I was playing golf with a friend this weekend and she was having a great round. She made a hole in one. It was actually the second hole in one of her life.

"When I asked her how she was able to do that twice she actually said, 'because I am a good athlete.' You see, not only did she feel she was a good golfer, she believed she was a good athlete. I am sure she thinks she had a blessed life as evidenced by her exuberant comment, 'wait till my husband hears what an awesome wife he has.' When we are hopeful, good things wash over us, bathing all parts of our lives."

Makes sense. "What about the enduring part?"

"The second part of hope is when we see good things as enduring or permanent. My friend actually said, 'I can't wait for my next hole in one." This significant event led her to believe that it will continue to happen even though the chance of the average golfer getting a hole in one is over 10,000 to 1. The chances of more than one in a lifetime are even higher. If you want to create hope, people need to believe that good things will continue to happen."

"Easy to say, but we have problems," I point out. "Layoffs, loss of business, people quitting and corporate asking us to cut costs. How do you create hope from that?"

She doesn't answer and lets me ponder my own question.

"I guess the opposite would be true for bad events then," I say, and she nods in agreement. "So we need to look at these bad events as more limited and temporary versus letting them become all-encompassing and lasting."

She grabs the marker and says, "Let's look at some of the beliefs you have up here and see where they fall. We will mark them based on whether they are all-encompassing or if they are more enduring."

We hit a roadblock on the first one because it isn't clear which category it would fall into. The statement says: "We can't get our act together."

Wow is that a downer, not very hopeful at all.

After some discussion we realize that it actually falls into both categories. It is a statement about the entire company when the problem was related to special orders. But it also implies that we will *never* get our act together.

"That supports Diane's point that these can be very subtle."

"—Which is why they can be very deep in our psyche too," Carolyn says. So we mark that item as both encompassing and enduring.

It doesn't take long to categorize a bunch of beliefs. The pattern that was so elusive becomes clearer; you can see how these thoughts can cut through the organization. There are times when people talk about one thing as the end of the world and a sign of imminent failure. Next thing you know, the energy is sapped out of the whole company and the foundation starts to falter.

However, there are some beliefs that don't fit into either category. "What about these other ones that don't have a label of encompassing or enduring?"

The beliefs we couldn't label include statements such as:

> *"Do we have the right people in the jobs to meet our goals?"*
>
> *"Do I feel I am able meet my goals?"*
>
> *"We are the redheaded stepchild."*
>
> *"Are we able to compete effectively?"*

We both look at them together when the pattern leaps out at me.

"These all have to do with our identity."

All the uncategorized beliefs seem to point to how we see ourselves, our team and who we are as a company. If this is what we believe, it surely will hamstring any actions we take. "These are the types of things we tell ourselves that keep us from getting out bed in the morning. These are the types of things that make us want to pull the covers over our heads and pound the snooze alarm over and over like hammering a stubborn nail into a plank."

We decide that the missing category is "identity," and we proceed to label the ones that fit there.

We look at the flip charts together, and, like a pattern embedded in a painting it now jumps out at us once we see it. "Wow, thank you, that was very helpful."

> **!**
>
> **Some of the more subtle beliefs are about identity, who we are and how we see ourselves, both as individuals and organizations.**

Carolyn takes the last pull on her water bottle and starts to bounce back to her rounds, waving her air quality wand as she goes. I am more confident that we have cleared some of the toxins we have been breathing in.

I suggest to her that our next outing should be at my house for dinner with our spouses and kids. She agrees and I let her know Sandra will call her to coordinate dates.

The next day, I take our team through the handiwork from the previous night's conversation with Carolyn. We have a long discussion about the subtlety of our beliefs and the impact it has on our company and on each of us.

Diane chimes in, confirming: "I can see how we can do a better job building these beliefs when something good happens. I like how it gives us a way to describe these events and build a strong culture." She has written down the three ways that beliefs shape our culture: Enduring, Encompassing and Identity.

I share with the team my discussion with Carolyn around hope and the quote she shared about how hope lies at the intersection of enduring and encompassing. We engage in a lengthy discussion about creating hope in the organization, how important it is that we feel hopeful and how we need to help others find hope.

Diane says, "I always struggled with the word hope. Even though I like to fashion myself as hopeful, I never knew how to define it in a more tangible way."

She continues by drawing a box around Enduring and Encompassing and writes Hope.

Starting to waver a bit, she asks, "But what do we do if we don't have any reasonable explanation for one of these areas?"

Robert asks her to pick an example so we can work through it together. She shares an example of a new contract they were recently awarded from a customer they have never done business with before.

On the flip chart Robert writes the three dimensions and says, "OK, let's brainstorm what we might be able to say for each of these."

The team starts throwing out comments, which Robert says he will write in each respective category. Right after the first suggestion, just like Carolyn and me the night before, he finds that some might fit in multiple dimensions.

"We ran into the same thing last night," I say. "Even though it might fit in multiple categories, let's agree that whoever suggests an item picks the category that best fits."

The statements flow pretty quickly.

> *"We are on a roll" – enduring*
>
> *"Things are looking up for the company" – encompassing*
>
> *"We have turned the corner" – enduring*
>
> *"We proved we can kick that competitor's butt" – identity*

The list continues on until the group runs out of steam.

Diane asks, "Do I communicate all of this to them in email, or verbally? How do I cover all of this?"

The group processes her question and comes to the conclusion that the first thing we need to do is be very conscious about what we can say in each dimension.

Karen says: "Just being aware and more deliberate will help us start building these beliefs into our business, amplifying all of our efforts and the results we are trying to create. Heck, they will help lift our outlook too. Rather than trying to script out some all-encompassing statement, maybe we find times and places to blend it into the regular flow of our conversations—whether it is in a meeting, a phone call or email. It is probably more important to find opportunities to communicate these types of ideas deliberately into everyday life and do so at multiple points, multiple times, in multiple ways. My guess is that it takes being deliberate, specific and repetitive."

"Just being aware and more deliberate will help us start building these beliefs into our business, amplifying all of our efforts and the results we are trying to create. Heck, they will help lift our outlook too."

Robert writes that down on the flip chart. Beliefs are impactful when we are deliberate, specific and repetitive.

"Not to be a downer," Peter breaks in, "but what do we do when something happens that is less than positive?" I appreciate him not making his usual doom and gloom, the-sky-is-falling-type comment.

Karen grabs the pen this time and says, "Lets break that down. Do you have an example that we can use, Peter?"

"Sure, the new product that we have been working on is having serious reliability problems and it looks as though we are going to miss our launch date. I've been afraid to tell you all about it and let you down. My team is diving into bunkers and avoiding talking to anyone out of fear of getting shot."

Well, that is a tough one to tackle. I appreciate him having the courage to bring it up. I know the group is shocked and even disappointed, but talking about this is the best thing for the team.

Karen charges ahead. "Rather than jumping into super hero fix-it mode or lobbing hand grenades of blame, let's tackle our beliefs first. We've been here before and quite honestly we haven't really known what to say; and what we have said hasn't been very helpful in figuring it out." Karen creates the same three categories of Enduring, Encompassing, and Identity.

Diane sees the flaw immediately. "So do we want to talk about how missing the deadline is enduring and encompassing? That will be a lead balloon of hope." The group chuckles.

I smile and explain, "I think it is the opposite. Instead of being enduring, we want to talk about it as temporary, not permanent. We also don't want it to turn into something that encompasses everything we do, so we want to limit how broadly we project the problem with this one product."

Joe asks, "What about our identity, how do we describe that?"

I ponder out loud: "I guess we don't want people to internalize the problem to the point where they are hiding in the bunkers or feeling like the redheaded stepchild. Of course we need people to take ownership and accountability, but not to the point where they feel they are disempowered or incapable."

Diane adds: "We also don't want to sound like Mary Sunshine either. People will see through that and it makes us look foolish."

I agree with Diane and tell her I had the same conversation the other day with Carolyn. "I think we can convey a sense of realism that still allows for hope and promise going forward."

Karen moves us along: "So are we ready to tackle our beliefs around the product delay?"

Everyone agrees, but they have a little more difficulty coming up with ideas on this one. It's much easier to see the negative when something goes bad. However, as they continue, some momentum builds.

We create a pretty healthy list of statements and the group follows the same rule about picking a category for each statement, even if they overlap with another category. They even change the category label to fit.

> *"We can figure this out"* – Not Enduring

> *"We have a talented and committed group of engineers"* – Identity

> *"We have products to fill the gap until this product is ready."* – Encompassing, limited

My favorite was "We shall overcome." I think borrowing some hope from Martin Luther King Jr. is a good thing. Heck, the civil rights anthem provided hope against far greater obstacles than what we have to overcome. It keeps things in perspective.

!

"We shall overcome" is a great example of a powerful all-encompassing belief.

"The biggest challenge," says Peter, "is going to be catching ourselves and others saying things and believing things that aren't helpful." His comment isn't interpreted as negative, but rather as reinforcing our need to be vigilant.

"It would also be helpful to share with the team what we talked about regarding our beliefs, how to look at them more deliberately and why it's important. We can't just leave that to the team in this room."

Everyone agrees and Robert signs up to hold some coffee-clutch meetings about this overall topic. I know when he is done it will have some form, and function to make this part of our culture in a sincere and authentic way. I can see him creating some fun competitions, some simple tools and new conversations across the company.

We adjourn the meeting tired but refreshed. I am even more hopeful than I have been in quite a while. I can see that this will have an enduring effect on our culture, that it will impact all parts of our business and it will shape the identity of who we are.

I think this proves that I just drank my own Kool-Aid.

Epilogue

It has been a few months of drinking my own Kool-Aid and it is refreshing. I am not foolish enough to believe that I have the answer, but I definitely feel as though we've found a way to solve for the impact we are trying to achieve as a team. Not only do I feel we are creating something enduring, but I feel much more satisfied with the impact I want to have in my own job.

I also notice people formulating their own impact. Not just their departmental goals, but what is important to them. For example, I have watched the production maintenance team bring in high schoolers to show them the interesting work they get to do at our company. This isn't just for show and tell, but to build interest in the important trade of what they do.

Not everyone bought into what we were doing and some people who had lost hope left the company. What's been interesting is that when we hired in new people, the formula became part of interview process and how we on-boarded new people. It is becoming part of our language: how we think and how we work while allowing people to formulate their own work.

The formula itself is taking on a life of its own. Just like the theory of relativity has been used, applied, peeled back and explored by scientists since Einstein, I can see our teams doing the same thing with our leadership equation. As a matter of fact, someone in the company gave the equation a name:

e^xponential Leadership

Everything isn't perfect, it never is. Our growth is not happening at the rate my boss wants. He is still breathing down my neck for "the numbers."

But now the conversations are different. We have very robust discussions about how to meet our investors' needs (something we can't forget) but we also temper the immediate demands with the longer view of the business. He even has adapted our quote, "Cash is King. Culture Trumps All." I know he respects what we have done because he has asked other divisions to do a site visit at our plant to learn from us. I watch our team beam with pride as they show off what they have done to create greater focus, build think tanks, break down silos, get people out of the bunkers and ultimately shape our culture.

> *Create greater focus, build think tanks, break down silos, get people out of the bunkers and ultimately shape the culture.*

I am continually appreciative of the role Carolyn played in helping me work through this, and it is time to say thank you.

Megan and I schedule a Sunday afternoon and evening with Carolyn and her husband Bob. The kids are invited and Carolyn's older daughter helps us herd all our cats and kittens, supervising both our two kids and Carolyn's younger two. All are excited and a bit rambunctious. It is heartwarming to watch them, and to share adult conversations and beverages with another couple. It's also gratifying to share time with the two true friends who have supported Carolyn and me so heartily in our business endeavors.

Spring has finally sprung, which means we get to sit on the back patio as the children play on the swing set and in the playhouse. Our conversation is light and personal, no talk of work. In fact, we find so many connections in our interests and backgrounds that it feels as though we've been friends for many years.

As dinner approaches, we grill out and feed the kids first because that requires all the adult hands on deck to prepare plates, chop food and, lastly, deal with the resulting mess. After the kids have eaten, they are fully fueled and rush back to play out the day's final hours of sunlight. Seated on the patio, we chat pleasantly while we enjoy our dinner.

After a satisfying meal I turn the discussion toward the late night conversations with Carolyn and our hike through the gorge. I share with Bob how appreciative I am of the time Carolyn took to talk with me, guide me and challenge my thinking. I explain that her involvement has had a profound impact on me, for which I am truly grateful. Though I know my comments make her feel awkward, I persist, continuing to explain how her impact has extended well beyond me. She has impacted every person in that company, I insist, by supporting the work we have all done. I would even say that she has affected this community by her contributions.

She smiles, admonishing me: "Now Jeff, don't you think that is taking it a bit too far?"

I respond, "In all seriousness, I am not."

It's then that I share a conversation I had with my boss three months into the job; one I hadn't shared with Carolyn before, nor with anyone on my team and not even with Megan.

"I had to confess to my boss that we were taking on water and sinking slowly, something that was very hard to admit. I also admitted I didn't know where to go. I knew we had an action plan, but I also sensed a hole somewhere I couldn't find."

Although my boss was a good guy, he could be very direct with me. "Well Jeff, you need figure it out for yourself," he told me.

This took place when Carolyn and I were only halfway through the equation. My boss also said the board did not have the patience for a slow grind of losses and decline, so I had to decide if I felt I could figure it out on my own. If not, I needed to tell him right then and there, so they could cut their losses by shutting down the division and writing them off. I can tell by the look on everyone's faces that they are shocked at this revelation, and even I'm surprised that I said it out loud. I take a deep breath and shift the direction of my little homily.

"If I hadn't had the opportunity to think this through with you, I think I would have told him, 'OK, shut it down,' I continue I say to Carolyn: "But you helped me begin to believe I could figure it out myself, even though I was very stuck. In my search for a secret and magic formula, I realized they don't exist. You helped me find a way to solve for results, or more importantly results with a lasting impact. Without our late night conversations, your questions and your insights, I don't think I would have gotten there on my own."

I pause for a moment while I let Carolyn drink in the importance of what I had just said.

"That is why I got you *this*," I finish, pulling out a surprise gift from under the table.

Of course Carolyn immediately says that I "shouldn't have," but I can't help but smile as I watch her unwrap my surprise.

> *"I was very stuck. In my search for a secret and magic formula, I realized they don't exist. You helped me find a way to solve for results, or more importantly results with a lasting impact."*

As she pulls out the object in the box, wrapped in fine tissue paper, I explain that Megan had inspired me to have this token of my appreciation made for her. It's a fine piece of decorative crystal, etched on one side with a picture of Einstein and his famous theory of relativity $E=MC^2$. As Carolyn admires the craftsmanship, turning the crystal over and holding it up to the dwindling light, I continue, "I know how much this equation means to you. By sharing it throughout our conversations, it, and you, obviously had a tremendous impact on me."

As she turns it over, she sees on the opposite side of the crystal the leadership equation we created:

$$R = (A * I)^B$$

"I wanted to share this with you because of your impact on this equation," I say. "I was inspired to read up on the history of the theory of relativity. Although credited to Einstein, there are so many people that contributed the knowledge that led to its discovery, from Sir Isaac Newton, to Marie Curie and so many other names lost to history. The theory of relativity has, and still does involve so many, many people. Which is also the case with our own theory and your significant contribution.

"It is my hope that people may see this equation and realize that although mysterious at some levels, leadership is indeed something we can theorize and quantify.

"I also predict that our equation will find a way to inspire others in the future to explore and discover their own leadership ability.

"I hope you can appreciate, as I do, how much you have impacted that. I am certain that all those conversations of ours in the late night hours at the office will reverberate beyond us from here on and contribute mightily to people's capacity to be great leaders."

By now I can see how thoroughly I've embarrassed her! But embarrassed her in a *good* way, surely. Bob's been beaming more and more with pride at his wife, recognizing, I am sure, what a bright and competent woman she is, but perhaps only now fully realizing what she had achieved through our conversations.

To alleviate a bit of the serious tone of my little homily, I tell Carolyn there is more, directing her to an envelope in the box, which she pulls out as Megan sets the scene. "Jeff and I wanted to do something special for you and your family," she says.

As Carolyn opens the envelope, Megan says, "Jeff shared with me that you love your time at amusement parks and zoos with your kids." To that end, we purchased an annual pass to our local amusement park and also a lifetime membership to our local zoo for your entire family."

Clearly overwhelmed yet again, Carolyn protests that really, this isn't necessary. "The company already pays me to provide services in the building."

"This is from me, from us," Megan assures her. "You have helped us recapture time as a family. That will have a huge impact for years to come. So we wanted to give you something that will impact *your* entire family!"

Carolyn is speechless, and clearly thrilled, which makes me smile. It's exactly the impact Megan and I had wanted to have on her.

Megan then breaks the moment and suggests she and Bob clear the dinner things and allow Carolyn and I to enjoy a cup of coffee while watching the setting sun.

As we observe the beauty of the sunset, Carolyn finally speaks again: "Jeff, I am overwhelmed. I really don't know what to say."

> **"What we've done will help them solve how they can have an even greater impact on the world around them."**

"There is nothing to say," I answer, "except that we owe it *them*." I point my finger toward our kids. "What we've done will help them solve how they can have an even greater impact on the world around them, regardless of the paths they choose."

We sit quietly and contently, taking it all in.

The God Particle

Many months later, I realize I haven't seen Carolyn at the office as much as I used to. I have been getting out of the office at a more reasonable time, well before the late shift. I also know that she now has team members who cover the late nights she used to spend in our offices.

The good news is that we found times to periodically gather our families and integrate them with our close circle of friends. Still, we both agreed at one of our get-togethers that we seem to have less and less opportunity these days to wax philosophical about the ways of leadership in the world. We both miss these conversations.

That's why we are now standing at the trailhead of another path leading up through a gorge I have never seen before. Per usual, Carolyn has popped up and started to climb, with me lagging and doing my best to keep up. Although I'm in better shape than our last hike, I am still not nearly as fit as Carolyn.

I ask, in a kidding way, if we are going to be talking about primitive tribes and spirit worlds on this hike. She laughs and dismisses my lame attempt at humor. But as we climb, I ask if she continues to be interested in physics despite running a business in a totally different arena. She replies she is always reading things about physics; there is just so much to learn and so much she (and all of us) don't know.

She then tells me about a book she has just finished about something called the "God particle." I find myself immediately interested. I had actually recently heard of something called the Higgs Boson particle and ask if that is what she is talking about.

"Yes and no," she says, explaining that the Higgs Boson particle was theorized over 50 years ago but only recently discovered through experimentation. "It is sometimes called the God particle, yes, because it's a sub-atomic particle that could help explain how the universe works. The book goes further to talk about exploring a single particle that holds our universe together and allows us to see how this is all connected."

I'm able to follow her for a fleeting few minutes but after that, her words go way over my head! I smile and wonder, who reads this stuff for *fun*? I am able to interject a semi-intelligent question every once in a while but she is way, way ahead of me in both her pace on our hike and in her thinking.

After about an hour we come to a clearing in the gorge with picnic tables. Carolyn arrives some minutes before I do, with time enough in fact to pull out her backpack and lay out some snacks. As I finally catch up, breathing hard, Carolyn tells me to relax and take a break. Then she throws a question my way that really captures my attention.

"Do you think there is a God particle in leadership?" she asks.

Holy cow! Here we go again! My mind is suddenly blown trying to connect a physics discovery with how we lead and communicate.

As my mind starts to wrap around her question, I consider what Carolyn had told me during our hike—at least the parts I could actually comprehend. "Well," I say, "I guess there could be something that unifies and holds together leadership at a very deep level. Even though we have come up with this equation, I have this gnawing feeling there's much more to discover. So maybe, I guess I would say, ah, just maybe there *is* a God particle."

"I just find it interesting to consider these types of things," Carolyn responds. "It is kind of like a game or puzzle out there in front of us, left by somebody or some 'thing' to figure out. There always seems to be more to figure out, doesn't there?"

I respond with a contemplative yes. Then Carolyn packs up what's left of our snacks and ushers us back into hiking mode. Our conversation during our climb zigzags from topic to topic like the switchback trails themselves. One moment we are talking about family, the next career aspirations, then next the work challenges that we can never anticipate, the next how our businesses are doing. Of course theoretical physics gets woven in from time to time, thanks to Carolyn.

I begin to see that everything is somehow all connected. Even the path we're climbing is connected. This rigorous

> *"Is there is a God particle in leadership?"*
>
> *"There could be something that unifies and holds together leadership at a very deep level . . . Everything is somehow connected."*

hike and conversation together challenge me both physically and mentally.

"There could be something that unifies and holds together leadership at a very deep level . . . Everything is somehow connected."

Hours later we make it back to the bottom of the mountain and I am totally spent. But thankfully I am also invigorated. Departing the parking lot, we agree to make special adventures like this one a more regular activity. The many benefits more than justify any arduous challenges.

The next day at the office, Sandra encounters me in my thinking pose with my feet on the corner of the desk. She closes my door knowing I am having one of my "moments" of deep thought, my eyes fixed on the framed poster of the leadership equation hanging on the wall. Several departments, conference rooms and offices now sport a poster with the Exponential Leadership formula.

An interesting addition is a marker and a place to write next to each poster inviting passersby to jot down their own equations around this one. As with Einstein, a lot of thinking led to the Exponential Leadership equation, so the markers serve as an invitation to continue to unpack it as we explore together what leadership means.

By one of the posters, in the Human Resources conference room, someone had written an equation for trust. Next to the production floor's poster, someone had written an equation for accountability. Elsewhere, someone had even taken my quote "cash is king, culture trumps all" and turned it into an equation all its own:

$$Culture = Cash$$

I glance over from the equation to ponder a new challenge waiting for me on the whiteboard. Carolyn must have been making rounds again in our building, or maybe she snuck in just to torture me with more theoretical leadership. Written in what was clearly her handwriting was this question at the top of the board:

Invite others to continue to explore, unpack and define leadership.

"Is there a God particle of leadership?"

It is a mind-bending question, or as Carolyn would say, a puzzle for us to figure out. I admit that I have since spent more than a passing moment thinking about it. For over a week I've walked past her question or paused to consider it. I am as lost with her question on the whiteboard as I was on our hike when she shared the concept of the God particle.

If there could be a God particle that unifies all in physics, does that suggest there is something that can unify all of our thinking around leadership?

I'm about to give up when Joe walks in with a flash of inspiration in his eyes. We had talked about Carolyn's

God particle question and had tried to come up with something that connected leadership together at a deeper level. He too had been stumped. With that look in his eyes, however, I wonder if he's come up with an answer?

If there could be a God particle that unifies all in physics, does that suggest there is something that can unify all of our thinking around leadership?

"What is it Joe? Did you figure it out?"

"I think so."

"So don't leave me hanging, what is it?"

"The answer is in the question," he says cryptically with a grin, and then heads out for his next meeting. I am left standing here not knowing what the heck that is supposed to mean!

Frozen, I stare at the whiteboard while swirling his comment around in my head, over and over and over again. "The answer is in the question."

"The answer is in the question."

What could he mean by that?

A solid five minutes passes. Then suddenly a flash comes to me too! I get it! I grab a marker and write a prominent question mark underneath the equation in very large script.

Is there a God particle of leadership?"

The God particle of leadership could be the question mark! Questions allow us to explore, to discover relationships between what we do and the results we get. They help us find meaning and define the impact we want to have.

I leave my question mark for Carolyn to find. I know she is surreptitiously checking on my progress and thus will see that I might have discovered a God particle for leadership.

I leave my office, smiling as I think about carrying the God particle with me as I make my rounds, wielding the question mark like an axe. I chuckle to myself: let's go split some atoms and see what energy we can release with my newfound question mark. Maybe the question mark is a microscope that will allow me to look deeply and find ways to fuse matter together for a new energy source. Or maybe it is a telescope that will allow me to peer into the recesses of the leadership universe to discover its mysteries.

The question mark as a tool of the Leadership God Particle may help split work atoms to release new and more powerful energy, give us a microscope to look into the deep recesses of leadership or a telescope to peer into the recesses of the leadership universe.

However I use this question mark, it is now a tool that will create deeper understanding, more power and ultimately an even greater impact. I need to wield it with confidence of course, and with caution as I continue my journey of exploration.

I turn off my office light as I head out to make my rounds for the day. And continue my questioning.

A Final Thought

If you are reading this sentence, I am honored that you would immerse yourself in this story and allow me to share a part of my journey of discovery with you.

It is my hope that this book has given you an opportunity to think about the impact you want to leave and how you move towards creating that impact. I also hope that you use these ideas to continue your own journey of leadership. This book is not "The Answer," but a way to continue to evolve how to think about leadership. Maybe this inspires you to create formulas around your own ideas on how to create impact. In that way you can show others that leadership isn't necessarily the nebulous concept only understood by people destined for success.

Remember, one of our greatest tools of discovery is the question mark. Take the opportunity to ask yourself the tough questions about who you are, why you do what you do and the impact you want to leave on this world. Start there and help others do the same.

Most importantly, enjoy the journey.

As theoretical leaders, like theoretical physicists, we can continue to explore and ultimately evolve how we think about leadership.

About the Author

Doug is a highly sought-after speaker, seasoned facilitator and adviser on executive leadership, business communications and success planning. Since founding his own consultancy in 2002, he has advised more than 10,000 executives in a variety of industries at all levels in their respective organizations. Doug can be found in the board room, conference rooms and the front line. He is comfortable sitting one on one tackling tough topics or on a stage in front of hundreds of professionals challenging us all to leave a lasting impact.

Over his career, Doug has been praised for his work with such labels as "powerful keynote speaker," "engaging facilitator of executive think tanks," "skilled leader of workshops on contemporary business topics" and "expert guide in developing strategic plans that create lasting impact."

His passion can be found in this last phrase: "creating lasting impact." His mission has always been to assist his clients and their organizations in their quests to achieve such "lasting impacts". He is proud to have empowered leaders of all stripes in their pursuit of achieving amazing results for their customers, employees and stakeholders. It has always been Doug's belief that such a mission is the requisite catalyst for attaining this.

To that end, he works hard helping his client organizations align their teams around powerful strategic plans implemented by strong leaders. You make this happen, he maintains, by converting the focus of a team's thinking from short-term results to *long-term* impact. The name of Doug's company, after all, is Impact4Results, a moniker based on his own favorite quote: "Results are fleeting, impact is lasting."

This book is a heart string in Doug's journey to educate everyone on dependable and effective methodologies for producing authentic and durable impacts of their own. He wants all readers of this book to know that adding "author" to his personal list of accomplishments by completing this book has been at once arduous, challenging, frightening, exciting ... and satisfyingly sublime! He therefore appreciates your taking a look.

On the home front, Doug enjoys spring, summer, fall – and endures winter from his home base near Rochester, New York. He loves cycling and traveling with his wife Francine, daughter Emily and son David, all of whom, he insists, are central to all he does.

48317170R00113

Made in the USA
Middletown, DE
15 September 2017